I0776029

The U.S.
Presidential Election of 2016:
The Plutocracy Won

"And when I speak, I don't speak as a Democrat. Or a Republican. Nor an American. I speak as a victim of America's so-called democracy. You and I have never seen democracy - all we've seen is hypocrisy. When we open our eyes today and look around America, we see America, not through the eyes of someone who has enjoyed the fruits of Americanism. We see America through the eyes of someone who has been the victim of Americanism. We don't see any American dream. We've experienced only the American nightmare." —Malcolm X

Also by
Humberto Gómez Sequeira-HuGóS

Notes from My Mobile Brain

It Hurts to Feel

Socialism of the XXI Century
or the Anti-revolution
(Spanish Edition)

Nicaragua: The Dialogue Between
the Doctrinaire Priests and the Trustees
(Spanish Edition)

In Transition Towards Poetry:
Granada (Nicaragua), the Bourgeoisie,
and the FSLN
(Spanish Edition)

Visions of a Somnambulist
(Spanish Edition)

The U.S.
Presidential Election of 2016:
The Plutocracy Won

Humberto Gómez Sequeira-HuGóS

Image Credits

Page 5: *Portrait of Malcolm X* by Robert Templeton, from the collection Lest We Forget: Images of the Black Civil Rights Movement. Courtesy of Wikipedia

To Malcolm X

Contents

Preface

The United States presidential election of 2016 took place while the Democrat and Republican Government—led by the Obama brand of imperialist politics of Hope—sustained the plutocracy's wars at home and abroad against the dominated classes for the control of the State. The ruling class' purpose is seizing the State—through the corruption of Congress—to transform it into a weapon for conquering human beings, dispossessing, and enslaving them to debt.

The presidential election is the plutocracy's political war against the other classes to persuade them they decide the next Government. Wearing the toga of democracy, the ruling class votes as a common citizen for a President of its State. Thus, it maintains the regime with which it has ruled for 215 years.

With the illusion of the free vote, the plutocracy has replaced the electorate's will to exercise their power over the economy, the State, the Congress, and the decision to go to war. The President can—with the support of Congress— use the Public Treasury to increase the military budget to fund the ruling class' aggressive power without the democratic voters' consent. Thus, the presidential election becomes a patriotic parade that satisfies the emotion caused by war, but not the need of the voters to live in peace and progress.

The plutocracy has conditioned the presidential election to its need to make war to keep its animal instinct alive, and the transference of it to the dominated classes in the form of patriotic enthusiasm. Using their war propaganda machine, the bankers and weapons merchants have converted war into a Government institution and a necessity of life. They have injected this lie—with the needle of the State—into the veins of the electorate. The freedom of voting is the result of military success: this is the lesson the new generations of soldiers are taught to prepare them for carrying on the tradition of making war.

The politicians, intellectuals, generals, political psychologists, and preachers of the "Kingdom of God" have converted the murder of a human being by another into an act justified by the "Love for the Motherland." She is the mother of the free and the brave who feeds on "martyrs" as a Cannibal God. When the electorate transforms itself into democracy and uses it to eliminate the institution of war, the presidential election will cease to be the contest in which the bankers and weapons merchants bet for the candidate who supports war as an imperialist tradition decorated with the myth of American exceptionalism.

The ruling class has conquered the State and converted it into its propaganda, censorship, espionage, persecution, and war machine. The end of the State is not the peace, or prosperity of the nation that supports it. The State subjects the presidential election to the plutocracy's end. War is the end towards which the capitalist and sacerdotal class are leading the dominated classes—using their children as the cannon fodder—to maintain the faith in the imperialist dollar and God.

In God, We Trust is Wall Street's war prayer. The Church imposed on society's mind the "holiness" of war with obscurantism, terror, and carnage. War doesn't sanctify murder nor does it immunize the murderer from the psychological horror it causes. Raising the decapitated head of a war victim as a victory symbol only satisfies the predatory pleasure of the plutocracy. This class of cannibals animalizes the society it consumes, sheltered under the Canopy of Divine Providence and Patriotism.

The presidential election is the plutocracy's ritual in which the electorate receives the host in the form of a flag imprinted with the confession "I Voted." Thus, the master reaffirms its position as the embodiment of democracy in the slave's mind.

Humberto Gómez Sequeira-HuGóS
Los Angeles, California, U.S. | December 26, 2017

Acknowledgement

I acknowledge María del Rosario Aguirre Durán, my life partner, for cultivating our friendship with her word and passion, and, thus, motivating me to write.

Prologue

The crisis of humanity consists in the belief in God and the State as entities that are susceptible to its cry for protection from the bourgeoisie's continuous war of dispossession which the State executes on their behalf with the public power of the courts and the armed forces.

All Hail the New Emperor!

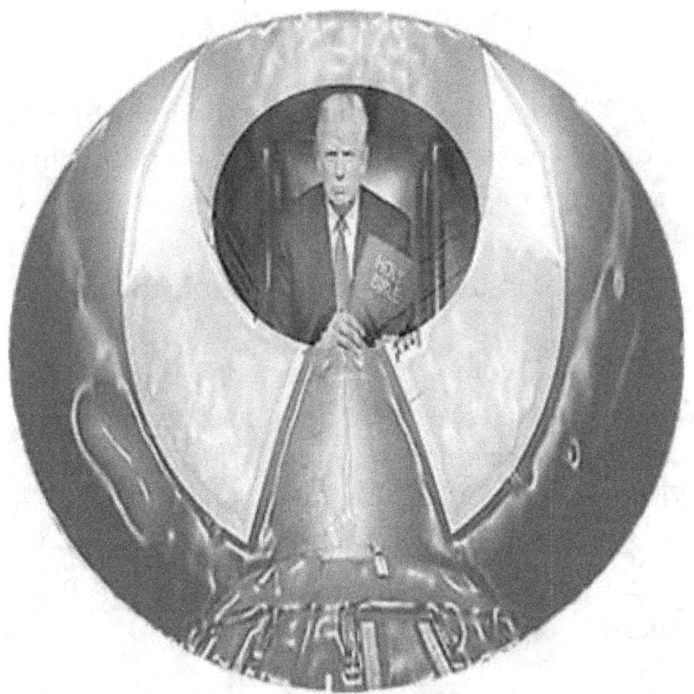

"And, again, I want to thank the evangelicals. I will never let you down," he said. [1]

Long Live the New Sacrificial Lambs!

And the crowd roars, passionately, each time their newly elected Emperor—who wears a golden pompadour—entices their patriotic and

---

[1] "Trump shows off family Bible, touts 'Christian values'" - TheHill

religious pride, exalting the armed forces, despising the "poor," and promising them national salvation, so help him, God.

Lost in their euphoric ovation, the State's and the Church's tributary slaves do not realize that their Emperor is preparing them as the new sacrificial lambs of the hungry predators who congregate in the Wall Street Temple to feast.

The voters who elected Donald John Trump as their President demonstrated that they lack political consciousness, admire the Plutocracy, and believe that their vote is an investment in their existential purpose with the sterile, opulent, and brutal lifestyle of their rulers.

Said election also shows that the State has succeeded in replacing the voters' will to power with the ruling class' myth of the white superhero, gifted with the spirit of "American Exceptionalism" as their amulet.

The Plutocracy Won

John Donald Trump and Barack Hussein Obama II. Their interest is the same as their predecessors: keep the State as the scepter of the plutocracy's power.

The wage slaves who vote in the election for President of the masters' State renounce themselves as the agents of their claims and the revolution that they need to make to fulfill them. The masters control the election with their idea of free enterprise as the condition of democracy; their propaganda machine; the bribery of the candidates; and the support of their business agents in the Government.

In the election process, the wage slaves are the objects of the illusions—faith, patriotism, democracy, and fear of the "foreign enemy"— with which the masters' candidates guide them to vote against themselves. Their acceptance of said illusions in exchange for their real interests—freedom, equality, justice, peace, and prosperity—is the reason they entrust their claims to the masters' business agents. In return for their trust, their class enemies use their votes as the weapons that the masters use to fight against them for the absolute control of the State. The emotional dependence on the State, as the protective *Uncle Sam*, has enabled the masters to fuse the wage slaves' interests with capitalism, totalitarian democracy, and the for-profit wars.

The submission to the masters' rule is the condition of the existence of the voting system as a democratic spectacle in which the exploited and the exploiters participate as friendly compatriots with the same purpose, that is, the preservation of the masters' system of slavery: capitalism and democracy. That abnormal relation, between predator and prey, is the result of the wage slaves' historic defeat by the masters' forces in the class struggle. The State destroyed the wage slaves' rebellious spirit by terrorizing them, eliminating their organizations, and declassing them. Without the power of their class consciousness, the State forced them to continue to be the masters' prey in the economy and cannon fodder in their war fronts. Thus, the masters confirmed themselves as the conquering class with the right to own the country they stole and the wealth that they extract from the exploitation of the wage slaves.

The wage slaves do not oppose their fusion with the masters who consume them and discard them. They support the masters' political parties and labor unions that cultivate their bondage. In the class warfare for the power of the State, the exploited do not differentiate themselves from the exploiters with their political party, program, or anthem. Adversely, they participate in the election as patriots of the country that the masters pillage, and vote for the candidates who embody their corruption.

The corruption of the wage slaves consciousness is the central reason the masters can maintain the illusions with which they dominate them. The masters' propaganda machine tells them that they are not slaves, but free citizens with equal rights under the Constitution of the country that the masters founded as their fiefdom.

Furthermore, the illusionists who are the *vox machina*—clergymen, senators, generals, broadcasters, teachers, labor union bosses, and clowns—convince the wage slaves that they can have rights only in capitalism for it is the spirit of freedom of the American democracy. They cultivate the illusions with the infertile seeds of faith, patriotism, and pride.

In the absence of the wage slaves resistance, the masters have been able to replace their dignity with their trinity of immorality, which is exploitation, profit, and war. The wage slaves do not see the masters as their enemies, that is, as the thieves who stole their means of survival, appropriate the product of their labor, and use the power of the State and the Church to keep them enslaved. They regard the masters as compatriots with whom they share the same homeland and existential purpose, equally. In reality, this is an illusion that obscures the masters' nature as predators who live off the wage slaves' energy.

The reason of the wage slaves' abnormal relation with the masters is, in part, their emotional attachment to the meaning that the masters infused on the noun America, the country they patented as their private property, as "the land of the free and the home of the brave." Besides, the lack of ideological independence and political power in the struggle for survival produced the submission of the exploited to the exploiters' democratic oppression system. These are the reasons the masters' business agents can use the wage slaves' votes as the weapons with which they executed a *coup d'état*. Consequently, they have replaced the principle of democracy—a *Government of the people, by the people, and for the people*—with the masters' existential condition: "We are the State and its purpose."

Entrusting their life demands to the masters' Democrat and Republican overseers, the wage slaves agree to the terms of their slavery system, Constitution, and Government. Under those conditions, they must remain dispossessed throughout their generations; accept wages that are not equal to the value of their work; live in inequality, and die with their soul indebted to the company store.

The wage slaves who participate in the election that the masters control contribute to the maintenance of the State as the masters' scepter.

Submitting to the restrictions—of life, liberty, and justice—that the State imposes on them, they defeat themselves as the subjects of the revolution that they need to make and continues to be the requirement for their emancipation. So too they negate that the masters are their enemies (not their kinfolk) whose only purpose is to exploit them to convert their energy into surplus value.

Using the State, the Church, obscurantism, totalitarian democracy, and the state of siege as their weapons, the masters are exterminating the wage slaves as the class of the producers of the values—ideas, goods, services, art, and interaction—that society needs to sustain itself and progress. Without their emancipation as the result of a social revolution, society cannot extirpate the cause of its crisis: the masters' control of the means of production, the State, and society's vision of itself as a commodity and consumer of commodities.

The masters are a gang of predators whose animal instinct restricts the use of their power to hunting to maintain it and expanding their hunting ground. They have divided humanity and the Earth according to their rapacious needs, using the State and the Church as their dividing weapons. Consequently, they do not have the social sensibility which is the capacity needed to build an egalitarian society.

The vote under the masters' dictatorship, whose official motto is "In God We Trust," has not produced the advancement of society to altruism. This state of consciousness is the condition for society's preservation through the achievement of freedom, equality, justice, well-being, and peace. Furthermore, the absence of a revolutionary class in society, acting as the altruistic model of living socially, explains the animalization of humanity under the dictatorship of ignorance, avarice, hate, and war that the masters, the politicians, the military, the intelligentsia, and the clergy preside.

The Trumpurification of the State

The election of Donald John Trump, a self-defined businessman, as President of the U.S. was the victory of the plutocracy that invested in his political campaign to seize the State to reaffirm their entitlement over it.

Since the Trump Brand occupied the Executive Office, he started to transform it into the tool for fulfilling the demands of the plutocracy which is his class and the interest of his Government.

The plutocracy's strategic demand is the purification of the State to adjust it to its predatory purpose as the robber of the nation's means of production and insatiable consumer of people and profits.

Therefore, the Trump Brand Government has taken the following actions to satisfy the plutocracy's need for being the State and its purpose:

- Specifying the racial identity, class, religion, and purpose of the State as the plutocracy's scepter.

- Designating the "poor" as unable to govern.
- Destroying the people's institutional power, pillaging the Public Treasury, decreasing the social budget, increasing the war budget, and disposing of the public land to enable the capitalists and bankers to exploit it.
- Militarizing the rule of law and overruling the habeas corpus.
- Censoring the truth and defaming the truth teller.
- Blaming the undocumented workers for the ruling class' crimes.
- Impoverishing the majority to enrich the minority.
- Using the State as the plutocracy's propaganda, censorship, espionage, persecution, torture, and war machine.

Thus, the Government is reaffirming that the State is the ruling class' sole property, judge, and executioner.

War and Capitalism

War is the praxis of the maniac desires for wealth and power of the usurers, arms dealers, pharmaceuticals dealers, generals, politicians, and popes. An ego made of ignorance, avarice, and hate possesses those classes of human primates. They feed it with the illusion of superiority, divine privilege, and an opulent and sterile lifestyle.

The war agitators have contaminated the veins of society's consciousness with their brutality and immorality which they inherited from their class predecessors: The liars and thieves who built their feudal estate with the blood and bones of the Native American Indian Nations and African slaves. This contamination has eroded truth, honesty, rationality and compassion as the pillars of society's Government.

War continues to be the inhuman method by which the plutocracy confronts its psychopathy and fear of freedom, equality, and justice for all. Their dread of being dethroned and ceasing to be a superior class privileged by God—is disguised by its political parties as free elections. The candidates are constructed by the plutocracy's propaganda machine as the forces of good and evil. Thus, the electorate is confused about the real problems that they need to confront and resolve.

In reality, said elections are the way in which the plutocracy fights against the other classes to keep its status of a predator of its species that dominates society. The result of this fight continues to be the enrichment of the plutocracy and its political lackeys, and impoverishment of the rest of the community. The real problems that the electorate needs to confront and resolve with the power that it surrenders to the administrators of the State—dispossession, dehumanization, and extinction by war—remain unresolved.

The inequality that is the base of the free elections is the condition of the plutocracy's existence, and its imposition is the end of a Government that has ceased to be from the people, by the people, and for the people. The Government now is the Chief Executive Officer that manages the business called country according to the plutocracy's war and profits agenda. The corruption of the Government and its appropriation by the plutocracy has produced the conversion of society into a commodity free of human moral concerns.

Dehumanizing society—through the practice of war and capitalism—the plutocracy has dehumanized itself and become a fierce predator of its species. This predator—which has appropriated society's means of production and pushed it to the financial precipice it created in 2008—is the real cause of war, dispossession, impoverishment, hunger, and illness that society needs to eradicate like a cancerous cell from its body.

However, the cancer of corruption has spread to the consciousness of the Government because the politicians to whom the electorate has entrusted their lives have exchanged truth and honesty for the plutocracy's values (brutality and immorality) which are the constitution of their domination. That is the reason political corruption continues to live in the body of society in a state of malignancy that produces suffering only. The truth is that the elections are part of the plutocracy's circus without bread in which the Democrat and Republican jesters try to entertain the starving masses to keep them economically, politically, and ideologically dispossessed.

The Demrepublican Charlatans

The Democratic and Republican presidential candidates are charlatans who lie to the electorate on behalf of political parties that cannot have an honest relationship with them and have never fulfilled the promises that they have made to them. They ask the electorate to vote for them as individuals based on likeability opinion polls, nationality, faith, and disposition to push the nuclear war button.

None of the proud-to-be-American candidates' promises to eradicate the capitalist system whose base is ignorance, selfishness, avarice, competition, dispossession, hunger, dehumanization, insecurity, hate, and war. The plutocracy conquered the candidates' hearts and minds and stole the power of the State from the people with the profits produced by capitalism.

The ruling class continues to use the power of the State and its propaganda machine to distract the nation from the truth. The Military Industrial Complex (MIC), Wall Street, Monsanto, Big Oil, and Big Pharma are the predators who are eating the nation alive, not the immigrant workers.

The capitalist class converted a lie into truth to enshroud its immoral character as the thieve who stole the land from the Native American Nations and baptized it as its country. One of their lies is that the so-called freedom of enterprise justifies the exploitation of a human being by another and the appropriation of the value that the exploited produces with its energy. Exploitation is the base of the ethical model that the plutocracy conforms and politicians follow with loyalty.

The ideologues, politicians, and priests—who function as the plutocracy's propaganda machine—have corrupted patriotism by equalizing it to capitalism, and converting war into the only way in which the human being can demonstrate their love for their motherland. The propaganda machine operators inject the lies in the mind of the soldiers that they use as cannon fodder to make war against the ruling class' designated enemies.

Truth is not the categorical imperative that governs the conduct of the capitalist politicians who promise a prosperous and secure future to the electorate. Their net worth, desire to increase it, and need to protect it are the conditions that drive them to serve as the capitalist class' ideological shock force. The umbilical cord that unites the politicians to their bosses is the lie that capitalism is a democracy and, therefore, is the only system in which the human being can be free.

The politician's relationship with the voter is the same as the capitalist with the worker. The capitalist uses the worker as the source of the energy that he needs to obtain surplus value in exchange for a wage. The politician uses the voter as the source of the belief that he needs to get a vote in exchange for a promise. The capitalist and the politician cannot have a different relationship with the people they exploit for the same reason that the wolf cannot feel compassion for the sheep.

The Democratic and Republican politicians belong to the caste of the house lackeys in charge of defending their masters' white house. In spite of the fact that the founding plutocrats built it with the blood and bones of the Native American Indians and African slaves, the lackeys admire it as a Mecca of imperial politics, money, and nuclear power.

The vote that the plutocracy's presidential candidates ask for will not be the instrument that they will use to make us "stronger together" or "make America great again." The corporate predators that Clinton and Trump represent have kidnapped America and stolen its resources and Government armed with nuclear weapons. Their only interest in America is exploiting it until it is exhausted and collapses. In reality, the America that said candidates refer to is the class of the plutocrats whose imperial, immoral, and sterile lifestyle they admire.

Let's free America from the deadly chokehold that the plutocracy has on it with the collaboration of its Democratic and Republican lackeys!

Let's restitute America—its resources and Government—to the Native American Nations, the African American Nation, and the people who work to sustain it!
Let us disarm the Military Industrial Complex, and Wall Street!

Let's turn off the lying propaganda machine!

Let's stop the persecution of immigrant workers!

Let's embrace all the nations of the world!

We, the people, do not have enemies! The Vietnamese people were never our enemies! The bankers, the oil barons, and the war weapons barons are the ones who make enemies by waging war against other countries to conquer and pillage them.

No more lies!

No more wars!

Voting Strengthens the Plutocracy's Ability to Wage War

The voters vote to renounce themselves as the agents of the revolution that they need to make to free themselves from the voting system in which they are the objects of the illusions—God, country, and democracy—that the plutocracy's propaganda machine disseminates to manipulate their mind.

The submission of their will to the State—controlled by the plutocracy that sits atop the Electoral College pyramid—strengthens the ability of the usurers and weapons merchants to make war against their enemies to satisfy their imperial ambitions of wealth, domination, and vainglory.

The Mask of Democracy

"War is peace. Freedom is slavery. Ignorance is strength." [2]

Working class voters: wake up! Your mind has been sequestered by the illusionists to use it as the propeller of the propaganda machine with which they convert a lie into truth, war into peace, slavery into freedom, and evil into good. The illusionists are the Democrat and Republican lackeys of the plutocracy who owns the propaganda machine and is the appropriator of the most significant portion of the wealth that you produce with your work.

The plutocracy and their army of speculators drove you into the subprime mortgage crisis of 2007 and destroyed your lives. Instead of defending you from their scam, their congressional lackeys rewarded the scammers by approving the Emergency Economic Stabilization Act of 2008. Your elected Democrat and Republican Government officials took 700 billion dollars from your tax fund and gave it to

---

[2] George Orwell, 1984

the robber bankers without asking you for your vote; this is how they govern you.

The Wall Street pirates did not invest your tax money in your prosperity. On the contrary, since the Governments—led by their agents: George Walker Bush and Barack Hussein Obama II—bailed them out, they have grown wealthier by repressing your economic growth, armed with the minimum wage law and the free trade agreements approved by the Governments mentioned above. And yet, they want more money, and power. Driven by their insatiable avarice—upholding the banner of free enterprise or capitalism—the plutocrats continue to pressure their political lackeys to provoke another world war to kill more innocent people, divide the world, and pillage the resources of the defeated countries.

The collaboration between Democrats and Republicans as servants of the same master enables the plutocracy to continue to lead the political *coup d'état* against you: the people and supreme authority of the country. The plutocrats started their *coup* on December 12, 2000, via the Supreme Court's decision nullification of the results of the presidential election to crown their designated courtier, George Walker Bush, as President. Albert Arnold "Al" Gore, Jr., who was Bush's contender, and the Democratic Party he represented, submitted to the unprecedented legal decision that replaced the people, the voting system, the Electoral College, and democracy.

The robber bankers have bought out the legislative vote that you entrusted to your elected Democrat and Republican Government Officials and replaced it with their war economy agenda. Both political parties identify with the properties of their character—ignorance, avarice, hate, brutality, immorality, opulence, vainglory, and sterility—and their end is to serve and protect them as the model of American Exceptionalism and leader of the Manifest Destiny.

The appropriators of your country have corrupted your Government and converted it into the weapon with which they want to dominate or destroy the world. Their Democrat and Republican lackeys have turned your vote into a product of the propaganda machine that produces the illusion of democracy that you control. In reality, the voting system is the weapon with which the plutocracy has stolen your country, your vote, your Government, and your power.

You need to recuperate your power to reinstate your self-determination and save yourselves and your planet from being destroyed by the plutocrats. That is the burning question in this presidential election, not the lies that the propaganda machine's salespeople are telling you. The principal myth is that you are free and that your vote is the proof and the guarantee of your freedom.

Hillary Rodham Clinton and Donald John Trump—the Democrat and Republican presidential candidates—want to distract you from the truth: They are millionaires who used the system that they call free enterprise or capitalism, the Internal Revenue Code, and the Government's permissiveness to enrich themselves to join the 1% Imperial Club. Both believe that capitalism—whose end is the exploitation of a human being by another or a weak country by an imperialist country—is the generator of freedom, justice, and equality for all. But, in spite of the fact that you are the producer of the work-energy that ignites the engine of the capitalist machine and keeps it running, you have not attained economic equality because the plutocracy and its lackeys do not want to be equal to you. Therefore, they do not want you to have the financial, educational, nor political means necessary for attaining equality.

The purpose of the plutocracy's laws of private property of the means of production and minimum wage is to be the border and shackle that keeps you in the condition of wage slaves. Thus, you are forced by hunger, and State repression to be the sellers of the work-energy that the plutocrats convert into surplus value.

The wealth that Clinton and Trump have appropriated is the product of your inequality and exploitation in the pyramidal system of capitalism where they sit at the golden pinnacle. They do not have any class differences: ideological, political, or economic. Both are children of the patriarchal State that was built by thieves and liars on stolen land with the blood and bones of Native Americans and African slaves, and the oppression of women. Consequently, they do not recognize you as a member of their class, but only as an object of ideological and political exploitation. The appreciation of your value as the class that produces the wealth and provides the services that sustain the life of society and the recognition of your right to equality is not what stimulates them to want to be President.

The Democrat and Republican charlatans want to seize the power of the Government to serve and protect the power of the sector of the plutocracy whose interests they represent. Their only difference is the question of how to satisfy the plutocrats' incessant avarice: with a globalist or nationalist program of exploitation of the working class? Clinton and Trump cannot be equal to you; therefore, they cannot represent your class interests in a Government which their political parties took away from you.

The truth is that the immorality of the plutocracy, the corruption of your elected Government Officials, and the conversion of the people's Government into the plutocrats' executive office is the root of your growing impoverishment. Furthermore, State violence and the degeneration of the people's democracy into a system of "inverted totalitarianism" (as Sheldon Sanford Wolin defined it) are consequences of the lawmakers' emancipation from the people and accountability to them.

Your elected officials have become sales agents—dressed with the toga of democracy—who sell your vote to their plutocratic political campaign donors to maintain their war chests and live like plutocrats. The millionaire presidential candidates do not tell you the truth about the root of your condition but attempt to distort it suggesting a false cause and solution. The reason is that they are products of the plutocracy's system (capitalism) which functions on the principle *the end justifies the means*. Corruption is the all-American apple pie that the plutocrats continue to use to recruit the political lackeys it needs to misrepresent itself and its relationship with you and your country with a mask of democracy.

Millionaire Trump suggests that foreign pirates have stolen the greatness of your country and your security is being affected by an invasion of immigrants. Therefore, he tells you that he will make your country great again by building a wall around you and appointing you the fascist police who will persecute immigrants in a labor camp where you would be a free slave.

However, his Nazi deportation plan is not unique. His colleague, Brand Obama—called by immigration organizations the "deporter-in-chief"—has deported more than 2.5 million persons. [3] What will Brand Clinton do if she is elected?

Millionairess Clinton suggests that together with her you will be stronger. But the corrupted actions that she has taken as your elected Government Official have not freed you from social insecurity or the threat of another for-profit world war. How can she make you stronger being a political lackey of the Wall Street Cartel that bought her soul? If you elect her as your President, she will apply the same casino politics, *pay to play*, that she used when she was the Brand Obama Administration's Secretary of State.

Your real urgency is to confront the truth about yourselves as the consumers of the products of the propaganda machine, that is, the Democrat and Republican politicians and their lies. You accept these products without

---

[3] **"Obama Has Deported More People Than Any Other President" -abcNEWS**

questioning their integrity and class interest. That is the reason they have converted the people's Government into a kakistocracy.

You continue to condone the treacherous behavior of William Jefferson Clinton, George W. Bush, Barack Hussein Obama II, Bernard "Bernie" Sanders, Hillary Rodham Clinton and all their corrupt and warmongering predecessors. The Democrat and Republican charlatans use your vote to support the plutocracy's war against you in exchange for a campaign contribution and admission into their imperial court as favorite courtiers with your consent.

You sustain your country, your Government, and the plutocracy's and their courtiers' parasitic, imperial, and sterile lifestyle with your toil and tax. Furthermore, you sacrifice yourselves to pay for the wars that they make to expand their imperialist power. In exchange for your sacrifice, they continue to exploit the resources of your country as if it was their private plantation and dispossess you, dehumanize you, and leave you to die in the cold. They treat you and have treated you for centuries, inhumanly because they are not humane, and believe that you are a for-profit commodity subject to the law of their capitalist market. Therefore, when they decide that the exploitation of your life does not produce the amount of surplus value that they want, they expropriate you of your right to work and throw you off into the cold. Furthermore, that is the reason they prefer to exploit the work of persons, including children, in other countries where they have a corrupt and violent relationship with corrupt and brutal governments.

Your elected Presidents, George W. Bush and Barack Hussein Obama II, lied to you to convince you to entrust the management of your country and your life to them. But instead of fulfilling their deceiving promise of a government of freedom and prosperity for you, their respective political parties, Republican and Democratic, united to approve the Authorization for the use of Military Force Against Iraq Resolution of 2002 and launch the war of dehumanization and pillage against the people of Iraq. Their unity as political parties—rooted in and sustained by for-profit wars—is the reason the Brand Obama [4] Administration has been the continuation of the Bush Administration.

Like Bush, Obama has converted the people's Government into an army at the service of the for-profit war merchants who own the Military Industrial Complex (MIC). The Drone Wars—led by Obama in Afghanistan, Pakistan, Somalia, and Yemen—have produced millions of dollars in profits for the MIC and the killing of thousands of innocent people. Their Democrat and Republican lackeys continue to use your vote as their moral justification for the crimes that they commit defending you, as they claim.

Like Bush and Obama, the luxurious presidential candidates of the twin political parties—Republican Donald John Trump and Democrat Hillary Rodham Clinton—also want to deceive you into believing that they are morally different and can feel for you, and fight to solve the problems that affect your life. However, they are not telling you that they and the plutocracy they serve are the creators of your

---

[4] **"Brand Obama - The Implications of a Branded President" - Staci M. Zavattaro**

unemployment, homelessness, and lack of health insurance.

Your elected Democrat and Republican Government Officials support the increasing military budget to finance the for-profit war that they call the War on Terror at the expense of your growing inequality and impoverishment, and the suppression of your freedom. The millionaire politicians stab you in the back because they do not have an affinity with you and both act as brands of products of the plutocracy's ideological machine whose purpose is the same.

The politicians for hire want to keep your mind subordinated to the following illusions:

a) you are free under a Constitution that cannot guarantee your human rights,
b) you and the plutocracy and its courtiers are free and equal under the law,
c) capitalism is a democracy,
d) under capitalism, you are free to be rich or poor,
e) and your vote is your power.

Like the plutocracy's Democrat and Republican lackeys, the labor union leaders, pastors, the intelligentsia of the left and right, Stalinists, and social democrats are also lying to you. They are telling you to vote because it is your patriotic duty, like believing in God and supporting the for-profit wars. They do not tell you not to vote because they think that the voting system is yours, democratic, pure, and separate from the corruption that the usurers and arms dealers who control it cause.

The believers in the American capitalist democracy do not have a solution to the following problems that the plutocracy—with the consent of your elected Representatives and Senators—has created and are consuming you:

a) political corruption,
b) elimination of the people's Government,
c) privatization of the State,
d) reduction of the people's welfare budget,
e) increase in the war budget,
f) State's patronage of the for-profit wars,
g) planetary crisis,
h) and the destruction of society.

The lawmakers do not show awareness of the following problems as part of the crisis that the capitalist democracy they support is causing:

a) underpayment for the human value of work,
b) rent, mortgage, and loans enslavement,
c) uncontrolled cost of living,
d) forced unemployment,
e) impoverishment,
f) malnutrition,
g) hunger,
h) illness,
i) drug addiction,
j) suicide,
k) forced eviction,
l) homelessness,
m) prostitution,
n) crime,
o) mass incarceration of African American and Latino citizens,
p) privatization of the prison system,
q) exploitation of the enslaved inmate population,
r) racial violence,
s) the killing of innocent African American and Latino citizens by police officers without prosecution,

t) punishment of whistleblowers,
u) persecution of dissenters,
v) indefinite detention,
w) torture,
x) the decline of literacy,
y) animalization of society,
z) and incessant wars that have not produced peace or prosperity for you, but only profits for the plutocracy.

The truth is that the Democrat and Republican party do not have the integrity, independence, courage, or determination required to confront the plutocracy to recover the country, Government, power, and life of peace that they have stolen from you. Both parties believe that capitalism is a moral system that the plutocrats embody, sustained by their declaration of trust in God. They are not your compatriots whose interest is to protect you from the enemies that they make by overthrowing governments, killing innocent people, and invading and pillaging the resources of other countries. You are not the exception to the brutal rule they apply in their relationship with the working class in other countries. They are at war with you to replace you as the supreme authority of your country with a kakistocracy of liars, thieves, think-tankers, bank chief executive officers, warmongers, spies, torturers, and hitmen.

The Democrat and Republican agents of Wall Street solicit your vote only to keep the democratic mask over the inverted totalitarian regime with which they dominate you. In 2000, the Supreme Court replaced you as the supreme authority that should have decided, with your vote, who had indeed won the presidential election. The Court's assumption of absolute power to designate your President enabled the plutocracy's Bush Brand Government to invade Iraq, kill thousands of innocent people, and pillage that country's resources.

Your vote has not produced what you are entitled to as a human being, worker, and taxpayer. The reason is that voting is part of the mask of democracy that the plutocracy and its political lackeys put on to deceive you. Your vote does not directly determine who will be the President, nor the policies that the new Government will apply. Your education, employment, salary, housing, health insurance, retirement savings, social security, prosperity, and peace in your life will continue to depend on the plutocrats who are the appropriators of the means of production and Government that enforces their laws. The Wall Street buyers of your vote will allow you to vote for as long as you do not rebel against their power. When you rebel, they will rip off the mask of democracy, and replace it with a military dictatorship. [5]

In this presidential election, you are paying the consequences of the Brand Obama Administration's plutocratic policies of inequality, impoverishment, suppression of freedom, racism, deportation of immigrants, and wars for profits. Those are the results of your vote for the impression that his superficiality as a product of the plutocracy's propaganda machine caused in your mind.

You are the only one who can change your condition by revolutionizing your mind and repudiating the corrupt electoral system in which you participate. The plutocracy and their Democratic and Republican party lackeys manipulate it to perpetuate their control over

[5] At the time of the publication of this book the Brand Trump Government—composed of billionaires and generals—had attacked Syria and threatened to "totally destroy" North Korea.

your mind and the Government. Cut the umbilical cord of your dependence on said parties' lies and build your organization to recuperate your self-determination, power, country, Government, and ownership of your life, peace, and prosperity.

The Coups d'État

The Plutocracy's Profits Before the People's Welfare: The North American Free Trade Agreement

The House of Representatives and Senate executed a *coup d'état* against the people, on behalf of the plutocracy, passing the North American Free Trade Agreement (NAFTA) Implementation Act. The coup was signed into law by William Jefferson "Bill" Clinton on December 8, 1993.

The institutions of a democratic Government executed the NAFTA coup with democratic means to achieve an anti-democratic end: the conversion of the people's Government into the plutocracy's Chief Executive Officer (CEO). NAFTA was the inauguration of the Government as the legislator of the plutocracy's desire for world domination and profits. Furthermore, it was the precursor of the anti-democratic method—secrecy and fast-track legislation approval—that the plutocracy's Democrat and Republican lackeys used to approve the Trans-Pacific Partnership Agreement (TPPA).

The Supreme Court's Power over the People's Power: Bush v. Gore

The Supreme Court executed a *coup d'état* against the power of the people, on behalf of the plutocracy, on December 12, 2000. It ordered the halt of the Florida vote recount and unilaterally ruled that the plutocracy's Republican Party's candidates—George Walker Bush, for President, and Richard Bruce Cheney, for Vice-president— were the winners of the election.

The Democratic Government of William Jefferson "Bill" Clinton and the sector of the ruling class that the Democratic Party's candidates—Albert Arnold "Al" Gore Jr., for President, and Joseph Isadore "Joe" Lieberman, for Vice-president—represented supported the Court's ruling.

The plutocrats' twin political parties, Democratic and Republican, the clergy, the labor union bureaucracy, the left, the right, and the media accepted the Court's replacement of the people's power with its autocratic power.

The coup was executed by an institution of a democratic Government with democratic means to achieve an anti-democratic end: the overthrow of the people as the State and the principle of *Government of the people, by the people, and for the people* as the existential condition of democracy. The Court's decision did not make America exceptional nor more democratic. On the contrary, it enabled the Bush-Cheney Administration and their Democrat cohorts to make war against Iraq to exsanguinate it, conquer it, and steal its wealth.

The Usurers' Interest Versus the People's Interest: The Emergency Economic Stabilization Act of 2008

The House of Representatives and Senate executed a *coup d'état* against the people, on behalf of the usurers who caused the subprime crisis of 2007, bailing them out with, approximately, 850 billion dollars of the people's tax money. This coup was supported by the plutocracy's twin political parties, Democratic and Republican, and signed into law by George W. Bush on October 3, 2008.

The bailout was a consequence of the repeal of the Glass–Steagall Act of 1932 by the ruling class' Democratic and Republican lackeys, in 1999, under the leadership of William Jefferson "Bill" Clinton. This law had been established to contain the overflow of the usurers' greed and prevent them from consuming the country.

The plutocracy did not invest the people's money in the people's welfare. On the contrary, since it was bailed out, it has grown wealthier by repressing the people's economic growth and freedom, armed with the laws of private property of the means of production and minimum wage, and the free trade agreements sponsored by their Democrat and Republican lackeys in the Government.

The coup was executed by institutions of a democratic Government with democratic means to achieve anti-democratic ends: the superimposition of the plutocrats' life over the people's life and the conversion of the people's Treasury into the bankers' welfare fund.

The plutocracy replaced the Government of the people, by the people and for the people with the *coups* led by their Fifth Column in the Senate without tanks surrounding the White House nor Generals on TV announcing the start of a new democratic era. Thus, the usurers and arms dealers confirmed themselves as the feudal lord who is also the State, its law, and order.

The Dependence on the State

The voters vote to renounce themselves as the agents of the revolution that they need to make to free themselves from the voting system in which they are the objects of the illusions—God, country, pride, and democracy—that the plutocracy's illusionists who operate the propaganda machine use to manipulate their mind. The submission of their will to the State determines the capacity of the plutocrats—who sit atop the White House and the Electoral College—to dominate them.

Their dependence on the State as their *Uncle Sam* has produced the fusion of their interests with the interests of the class and political parties that control its functioning: the plutocracy and the Democratic Party and Republican Party. The working class and *petite bourgeoisie* (middle class) voters do not differentiate themselves with their political party, program, and anthem. They participate in the elections as patriots of a homeland—that the usurers have appropriated—who must make war: kill and be killed on her behalf to demonstrate their loyalty.

The plutocracy through the offices of their Democrat and Republican lackeys—who manage the State as their for-profit war machine—has captured the voters' vote and converted it into the weapon with which they executed a political *coup d'état*. Thus, the usurers' and arms dealers' lobby overthrew the voters as the embodiment of the principle of *Government of the people, by the people and for the people.*

Consequently, the ruling class has defeated the power of the people which is the condition for the existence of a real democracy.

Oppose the Robber Barons' War!

Citizens:

The robber barons [6] —the thieves who stole your country and Government—have turned on their for-profit war propaganda machine again, using the for-hire tongues of your elected Democrat and Republican Government Officials. This time they want to invade Syria [7] to commit the same crimes against humanity that they executed in Iraq, using your sons and daughters as cannon fodder.

The merchants of death lied to you, scared you, and used your fear as their platform

---

[6] "Robber baron, pejorative term for one of the powerful 19th century U.S. industrialists and financiers who made fortunes by monopolizing huge industries through the formation of trusts, engaging in unethical business practices, exploiting workers, and paying little heed to their customers or competition." -Encyclopedia Britannica

[7] Besides, on September 21, 2017, Trump announced at the United Nations that "The United States has great strength and patience, but if it is forced to defend itself or its allies, we will have no choice but to totally destroy North Korea."

to invade Iraq to exsanguinate it, conquer it, dehumanize it, enslave it, and steal its wealth.

The usurers and arms dealers want another war because they are a class of predators of their species whose instinct compels them towards the enslavement of humanity and appropriation of the world's wealth. Avarice and brutality are the reasons they incited the wars in Afghanistan, Iraq, and Libya.

Carnage, pillage, the animalization of the human being, and the destruction of the Earth are the only effects of their wars. Your humanity, wellbeing, prosperity, equality, freedom, and security are not their motives.

Their behavior, at home or abroad, is conditioned by predatory instinct, not by patriotic allegiance to you. That is why they are conducting the free trade war against you to discard you as the human reason and value of the national economy. The Brand Obama Administration, its cohorts of the Republican Party, and their Church support their desire for plasma and profits.

The robber barons' class includes the usurers who lied to you; sold you tricky mortgage contracts; stole your money; evicted you from your home; and pushed you into impoverishment, in 2007, with the consent of the Government that you support with your toil and tax. They used your Treasury to enrich themselves; buy out the vote that you entrusted to your elected Democrat and Republican Government Officials; and hired them as their White House lackeys.

Using their Representative and Senator lackeys as their Fifth Column in the Government, the usurers, and arms dealers executed a *coup d'état* and overthrew your sovereign power as the existential condition of democracy. Thus, you are no longer the embodiment of the principle of *Government of the people, by the people, and for the people.* Your defeat is the burning question that the plutocrats' Democrat and Republican agents, Hillary Diane Rodham Clinton and Donald John Trump, are not discussing on the talk show called the presidential election debate.

The Wall Street cartels who have stolen your country, economy, vote, Government, and peace have constitutionalized themselves as the people, nation, Government, law, and order with the blessings of the President, Congress, Supreme Court, Pentagon, and Church. Therefore, they continue to assault, dehumanize, and dispossess you of your human rights with impunity.

The robber barons are robbers, not patriots. Their interest is not your interest. They are the predators, and you are their prey. That is the real relationship they have had with you since their ancestors founded their State to legalize their loot and control your lives. Their purpose is not to contribute to your growth, but to destroy the roots of your existence. Don't believe their lies, nor let them make another predatory war. One more conflagration could extinguish humanity and the Earth, and would only create more suffering and hostility. Unite to recuperate your country, economy, vote, Government, and peace!

Soldiers: You are the sons and daughters of the mothers of the people who support the Government and you with their toil and tax. You are not a private army at the service of the usurers and arms dealers who live off the pillage of war. You are public servants whose mission is to serve and protect the people who engender and admire you. You owe your allegiance to the people, not to the thieves who have stolen the people's Government, and used its power to turn your fellow veterans into an impoverished, homeless, and ill class.

Do not kill or be killed making the robber barons' war! Stay home and unite with the people to recuperate the *Government of the people, by the people and for the people!*

The End (Power) Justifies the Means (Corruption)

"The atom bomb was no 'great decision.' It was merely another powerful weapon in the arsenal of righteousness."

Harry S. Truman tried to convert the bombing of Hiroshima and Nagasaki into a good that he did to the people of Japan because—as a Christian and President of the United States—he was righteous and, therefore, the bomb was his messenger of righteousness. However, the weapon was built with his consent, and the approval of the Democratic Party and Republican Party, knowing that it was "an explosive great enough to destroy the whole world." However, they decided to use it to their end—demonstrating the power of the plutocracy's new weapon to their enemies—justified the killing of thousands of innocent persons.

Truman's end was the same as the usurers' and arms dealers' purpose, that is, the conquering and pillaging of Japan. It was not the imparting of a lesson on righteousness to the Japanese people, particularly the women whom the soldiers who invaded Japan raped. His attempt to baptize the bomb as a force for good was the reaffirmation of the mentality that the authors of the Native Americans and Black Slaves Genocide: The end (stealing) justifies the means (killing) is the morality, the law, and the cornerstone of the free enterprise system or capitalism.

The robber barons built capitalism by killing Native Americans to steal their land and enslaving African persons to force them to work and appropriate the wealth that they produced. With the power that they acquired—converting the plasma of their victims into money—they hired the statesmen who constitutionalized their loot as their property. Thus, they established corruption as the condition for the achievement of the end of capitalism and the Government that defends it as a democracy.

The corruption of the usurers and arms dealers is the moral rule with which they have educated the generations of Democrat and Republican lawmakers who have administered the people's Government as their means to achieve their end. With the help of their political lackeys in the Government and propaganda machine, they have replaced the role of the people as the source of ethical inspiration, the means, and the end of Government. Furthermore, they have designated themselves as the end of democracy and converted the people's Government into their court.

The people's elected Democrat and Republican Government Officials have repudiated the people's aspirations of freedom, equality, prosperity, truth, justice, and peace as their values, and replaced them with the plutocracy's values: selfishness, avarice, corruption, hate, aggressiveness, opulence, sterility, and vainglory. Consequently, the officials use the power of the Government—which is sustained by the people with their toil and tax—to defend their profits as a social value.

Defending the private ownership of the country; private property of the financial system; theft of the wealth that the working class produces; suppression of the people's prosperity; exportation of jobs; free trade agreements; and making war to globalize the power, and profits of the plutocracy the lawmakers have become their servants.

The luxurious President, Senators, and Representatives—who feed on the people's Treasury—condone the capitalist parasites crimes against the people, lie, and punish those who tell the truth. The army under their command spies, censors, persecutes, represses, incarcerates, and tortures those who disagree with the new robber barons' proposition, *à la* Louis XIV, that they are the State, the people, and their purpose.

The Wall Street Cartel (WSC) and Military-Industrial Complex (MIC) converted democracy into a dictatorship corrupting the consciousness of the Government of the people. The President, Senators, Representatives, and Generals are the dictatorship's operators. Their interest is to satisfy the usurers' and arms dealers' need for national and global domination.

The subjugation of the people to the WSC's and MIC's power as mere tribute payers and the conversion of the Public Treasury into their war fund is part of the for-profit wars plan that the State is conducting to conquer and pillage the rest of the world.

The fusion of the Government with the interests of the usurers and arms dealers is the reason their Democrat, and Republican courtiers curtail the people's constitutional rights, approve their free trade agreements, conduct their covert wars, order the overthrow of foreign governments and the killing of the heads of foreign states.

The public officials have turned themselves into parts of an automated government machine that produces obscurantism, lies, political defamation, repression, patriotic and religious pretensions, imperial vainglory, brutality, intimidation, social conflict, and decadence.

Truman's hypocrisy is the new robber barons', and their Democrat and Republican courtiers' method for making the people believe that their government principle—the "good end" justifies the "evil means"—supersedes their corruption and validates them as the democratic leaders of the world they dominate. Keeping the people's mind subjugated to the acceptance of lie as truth; dishonesty as honesty; impoverishment as enrichment; dictatorship as democracy; slavery as freedom; and war as peace is the objective of the capitalist propaganda machine operators.

Hillary Diane Rodham Clinton and Donald John Trump are just the twin masks of the root of the corruption of the consciousness of the Democratic Party, Republican Party, Government, democracy, electoral system, media, clergy, intelligentsia, and academia. The root is the selfishness that is the stimuli of free enterprise or capitalism, a system that requires the exploitation of human beings and the Earth; and competition and war to produce the surplus value with which the robber barons sustain their imperial power and parasitic and infertile lifestyle.

Reasons Not to Vote

Citizen workers, know these truths:

The voting system is part of the wage system, and both are elements of the ideopolitical system that the bourgeoisie uses to dominate you with the power of the State.

Your vote does not bind the twin capitalist parties, Democratic and Republican, to the duty of forming a Government—of the people, by the people and for the people—of prosperity and peace.

The Democrat and Republican politicians use your vote as their credentials to occupy your White House as the lackeys of the Wall Street robber barons who contribute to their war chests and are the model of the immorality they share. They use your Government to rob you of your political power and human right to live in a state of social well-being.

The luxurious members of the House of Representatives and Senate, and their Big Lords of Money, Land, Oil, Drugs, and the Military Industrial Complex (MIC) converted the voting system into an inverted funnel through which they channelize your power. Thus, they take your vote as the proper validation of their corruption, imperialist ambition, and enmity against you.

Whoever of the modern robber barons' candidates you vote for will form a Government of Wall Street.

Brand Obama: The Grand Democratic Hope of Deception

Faith, as hope, is the illusion that the new robber barons' Democrat and Republican illusionists implant in the believers' mind to convert them into the saboteurs of the revolution that they need to make to free themselves from the illusion, and the illusionists and their masters.

Armed with the word Hope, the Brand Obama model of imperialist politics—invented by the modern robber barons' political think tank—intoxicated the believers with an almost sexual, à la Kennedy, desire. Enchanted by his Hollywood celebrity style, the believers allowed him to lead them as sacrificial lambs to the Wall Street altar, where the robber barons gutted them as they sang "We shall overcome."

Hope was the magic pipe that the Democratic Party propaganda machine used to lead the believers through a campaign of distraction from the human ruins created by the robber baron's predatory wars against their mortgage clients, and the people of Iraq. The Republican Party led these acts of dehumanization and pillage with the support of their Democrat accomplices.

The Great Democratic Hope of Deception—represented by Brand Obama—was a *coup d'état* against the people. It produced the auto industry bailout, the police State, the for-profit drone wars, the forced tribute to Big Pharma, the dispossession of the working class, the empowerment of the robber barons' class, and the conversion of the State into their legislative, and war machine.

Brand Obama was the window dressing of a violent campaign to eliminate the people as the owner of the State and enthrone the robber barons as the American Louis XIV, entrusted by God with the mission to become the State and the model of the people's aspirations.

As a deception created by the propaganda machine, Hope—in the hired tongue of Obama and his delegates—obscured the political awareness of the working class, and stimulated the conditions for the emergence of the Great Republican Wall of Hope in its mind.

Obama Is a Fake

Barack Hussein Obama II denounced the Fake News on Facebook and suggested that they undermine the U.S. political process during his press conference in Germany yesterday, November 17, 2016.

The real news is that Obama is a fake. As a graduate of the School of Fakism, he skinned the truth of the social condition he shares with the African American Nation—a descendant of the slaves whose blood and bones are the base of America—to sell himself as a political lab subject to the Wall Street robber barons. Their think tankers made him up into a fake marketable product of the artificial political values of the thieves who stole the country that they rent to their real tax-slaves as a phony democracy.

He is the real underminer of the U.S. political process as a part of the robber barons' Democrat and Republican propaganda machine whose function is to produce fake news to obscure the truth and cover up the corruption that is their creed and *modus operandi*.

The political process that Obama defends as if it was the moral circulatory system that determines humanity' life is the product of the modern robber barons' constant war of conquest and pillage in the U.S., and around the world.

Its base is made of the blood, and the bones of the magnificent Indians and African slaves that they killed to build their power and impose their immorality on the nation as patriotism.

Obama is a fake brand of democracy which, like a Big Brother, preached the Fake News of Hope to the flock of his admirers to seduce them, get their vote, and then lead them to their ruin.

A fake product cannot criticize another. Brand Obama and the propaganda machine of which he is a part cannot tell the truth for truth cannot sustain corruption.

The Great American Delusions

I read an article in which the author voiced the experience she lived as an object of racism in what she referred to as "Trump's America." She used these affirmations: "our country," "our future," and "our reputation" to refer to the America that she believes in and *The Accidental Emperor with the Golden Pompadour*—named Donald John Trump—is damaging in her view.

The people who say that they do not believe in the America that the Brand Trump Administration (BTA) represents invoke the America of their faith—the virgin mother of freedom, equality, and justice for all her children—to justify their disagreement with reality.

However, America the free from racism, and the people's claim that it exists for they feel they possess it is a delusion. Their argument that the BTA's racist policy does not represent the American spirit is not real. Racism and the brutality with which racists express it did not start in America on the day that American voters elected the owner of The Trump Organization LLC President of the United States of America.

Racism is the virus that the so-called founding fathers' ancestors brought to America. It was the motivator of the genocide they committed against the Native American Nations and African slave families. Thus, they established their destructive power which they enshrined in the mind of the survivors of their victims as the product of "Manifest Destiny," and their racial superiority.

The affirmations in question are components of the illusion that the thieves who are the constitutional owners of the country they stole implanted in the State's tax-paying slaves' mind with their propaganda machine. The Democrat and Republican Government Officials are the *vox machina* and sellers of the public trust to the new robber barons "for a few dollars more" in their war chests.

"Our country," America, is the brand that the thieves used to constitutionalize the land they stole from the Native American Nations. America is also the product of the thieves' exploitation of the African slave families who worked the land and produced the wealth that they appropriated.

"Our future" is a nuclear poker card in the pocket of the members of the Military-Industrial Complex(MIC) Cartel. The Brand Obama Administration (BOA) was, and now the BTA is the cartel's poker dealer.

"Our reputation" is the suffering that the thieves cause, at home and abroad, through their constant predatory hunting—including the for-profit wars that the State conducts on their behalf—to feed their insatiable appetite for money and political power.

The thieves' Democrat and Republican aids in charge of the management of the State defend their rapaciousness as "American democracy," aggressively, violating the people's democratic and human rights. Dispossession, dehumanization, hunger, illness, suicide, suffering, and the destruction of the human spirit and its element are the thieves' contributions to the country they claim to love. In reality, they are sensitive only to their ambition for wealth, political power, and imperial vainglory. They have converted their ambition into public policy with the vote of the lawmakers who are their agents in the House of Representatives and Senate. The policy is the Government's reaction to the thieves' desire to become the State, its religion, and purpose.

The BOA continued the process of elimination of the people's State. It increased the public debt and the war budget, kept the MIC for-profit wars around the world, decreased the social budget, enforced the legal foundation for a police State, censored dissenters, militarized the police, and deported immigrant workers and children *en masse*.

The leader of the *Government of Hope* for the dispossessed helped the dispossessors to appropriate a larger share of the nation's wealth, while he and his accomplices stood indifferently to the increase in unemployment, homelessness, hunger, opioid addiction, mental illness, racism, and police killing of innocent people.

"Trump's America" is the same as "Obama's America." For Trump and Obama, America is the nation that the Wall Street Cartel (WSC) converted into a for-profit commodity they trade. The WSC's purpose is to make their commodity "great" by increasing their pillaging of *America the working-class family* and her resources, fiercely and continuously. The BOA sustained the cartel's ownership of *America the for-profit commodity* by converting the Public Treasury into their welfare fund, and the State into their fortress and for-profit war machine.

On his inauguration day letter to Brand Trump, Brand Obama affirmed the indispensability of the "American leadership" that he followed according to the imperialist agenda of the Wall Street usurers to whom Brand Trump owes millions of dollars [8] and class allegiance. In part, Obama's letter to his colleague said the following: *"Second, American leadership in this world really is indispensable. It's up to us, through action and example, to sustain the international order that's expanded steadily since the end of the Cold War, and upon which our own wealth and safety depend."* [9]

Brand Obama and Brand Trump were elected by voters who believed their lie, that is,

---

[8] **"Report: Donald Trump's companies at least $650 million in debt" – CBS News**

[9] **"Exclusive: Read the Inauguration Day letter Obama left for Trump" - CNN Politics**

they were going to use the political power of their vote to fulfill their demands. The Brand Obama Administration didn't change the condition of the predatory relation that the imperialist cartel imposes on *America the working-class family,* that is, absolute freedom of profitmaking by any means necessary. On the contrary, it prepared Trump's emergence by expanding the State's anti-working class legal and military arms and pushing it deeper into a state of inequality and desperation. [10]

Trump is another son of *America the for-profit commodity* engendered in the womb of ignorance, avarice, hate, and indifference to inequality and social injustice. He is a member of the class of the profit predators whose reason for being Americans is to exploit the people and their resources. He does not have the qualities— wisdom, social sensibility or compassion—to be the President of a society in which the parasitic minority, the plutocracy, lives off the life of the working majority and rules with the scepter of inequality imposed by the State.

---

[10] **"During Obama's Presidency Wealth Inequality Has Increased and Poverty Levels are Higher" -CounterPunch**

"Businessman" is Trump's description of himself, that is, an expert in the immoral art of making a profit through the exploitation or suppression of the life of another supported by the State's Tax Law. Thus, he will treat America as a business on behalf of the owners he represents and superimpose their profit-making interest on the need of *America, the working-class family*.

Brand Trump has started to use the tools for constructing a dictatorship to maintain his class' power. The appointment of generals and billionaires to his Cabinet, the elimination of the people's Government, the increase of the war budget, the reduction of the social budget, and the proposed reduction of the billionaires' tax are actions that show the businessman's understanding of Government.

Misogynism, contempt for the "poor," obscurantism, lies, defamation, espionage, censorship, nationalism, religionization of the State, endorsement of police brutality, deportation of immigrant workers and children, and the threat of nuclear war are part of *The Accidental President's* government instruments.

The owner of the Trump Organization LLC also uses misrepresentation to mislead his audience into believing that his lies are "alternative truths." He glorifies his self as the Savior of the State, his stupidity as intelligence, his bruteness as gentleness, his mediocrity as excellence, and his misogynism as virility to transform himself into the State and its purpose.

His presidential campaign slogan, "Make America Great Again," was like any other advertisement that is intended to stimulate a person's mind to buy something, including an illusion. "Great" does not mean "equal." Rather, it is a suggestion of an attitude towards a country whose resources continue to be stolen by the plutocracy and are protected by the State as private property. The function of *America the private for-profit commodity* is to produce endless wealth for its appropriators. Thus, it has never been and cannot be humanely "great" because it is the product of the dehumanization of *America the working-class family*. *America the private for-profit commodity* is founded on the cartel members' ignorance, selfishness, avarice, privilege, opulence, aggressiveness, sterility, and indifference to inequality and injustice.

The "greatness" that the plutocracy wants to infuse into *America the private for-profit commodity* they own is an increase in the profits they extract from the inequality, injustice, and suffering they impose on *America, the working-class family*. The Trump Tower of ignorance luxury, meaninglessness, and confusion is the symbol of the plutocracy's ambition. "Great" is only an illusion that is part of the vocabulary that the Democrat and Republican operators of their propaganda machine use to suggest that it means a state of freedom, equality, justice, peace, and prosperity for *America, the working-class family*.

In reality, "great" means the rejuvenation the plutocracy's American sanguinary orgy of immoral, and unrestricted enrichment at the expense of the suffering of the majority of society that they have dispossessed. That American tradition was practiced with true Christian faith by Barack Hussein Obama II with the help of his Democrat and Republican accomplices. Brand Obama's Hope was the grand American delusion that now Brand Trump's anti-immigrant worker U.S.-Mexico Wall represents.

Political corruption, the privatization of the State, and the endless enrichment of the WSC through the creation of poverty and the Police State are the *America the private for-profit commodity*'s traditions that the BTA inherited from the BOA who inherited it from the Brand Bush Administration. Corruption is the force imposed on the State by the WSC's Chief Executive Officers who design the public policy of unemployment, homelessness, hunger, illness, racism, violence, and wars of conquest and pillage.

The members of *America the working-class family* who support the State—which the new robber barons use as their shock force to oppress and repress them—do not have a country. The bankers and landlords who are the owners of *America the private for-profit commodity* have expropriated their lives, jobs, homes, society, Government, and dignity. *America, the working-class family,* will have a real country when they revolutionize their minds, break the illusion, repudiate the illusionist, think like a class, organize themselves into their political party, and take their power back from the thieves who stole their country.

Epilogue

The Messianic Promise

The messianic promise of capitalism held by the capitalist class' *vox machina*—that it can generate freedom for the wage slaves has not come true. Neither have the workers who are the sellers of the energy that keeps the capitalist machine running attained sustainable wellbeing as a result of their labor.

At the juncture in which the capitalist class has seized the power of the State and is waging war against them, the slaves' burning task is to free their minds by disbelieving the capitalists' lie, that is, that they have a common interest in the system that is pushing them into extinction.

Ideologically free, the working class will be able to convert the energy they produce into awareness of their interests, predicament, and need to save themselves from becoming an extinct species as a result of capitalism's ravaging force.

The producers of society's wealth evolved from the transformation of their instinct into the power required to overcome the adverse force of the ruling class and survive. The capitalist class has taken away their ability, weakened them with faith, enslaved them with patriotism, stopped their evolution, and submerged them into a mortal crisis propelled by their for-profit trade and military wars.

The capitalists' messianic promise is an illusion that the operators of their propaganda machine sustain with lies, obscurantism, defamation, and intimidation.

The masters cannot emancipate the slaves for they are the condition for their enslavers' freedom.

The Antithesis of Freedom

"Whose side are you on?" "Don't you love your country?" [11]

Nationality, like religion, is the brand that the State impresses on a person's forehead to identify the Feudal Lordship to whom they owe allegiance and tribute for having been born within his fiefdom. It is not one of the human primate's natural properties, such as freedom, which animated their evolution on the open field of nature when they lived without a passport. Then, nationality was not a condition for living for the State that created it as a condition for its functioning did not exist.

The root of nationality as a political brand is in the relationship that the feudal lord imposed on the serfs that he exploited. The serfs worked his land for his *beneficium* in exchange for his protection from his enemies. But when the lord engaged in war, he used the serfs as the fodder for his cannon. The State upheld the lord

---

[11] "Full Metal Jacket." A 1987 British-American war film directed and produced by Stanley Kubrick.

---

as the benefactor and the serfs' allegiance to him as their benefit. Today, nationality is the bond-servitude that subjects the human being to the State and, consequently, to the plutocracy, the new feudal lord it serves.

Citizenship is not a condition for the human primates' existence, identity, or freedom. On the contrary, it is the negation of human as identity and the codification of liberty, i.e., the Constitution, The Pledge of Allegiance, Tax Code, and the USA PATRIOT Act. [12] Liberty is an expression of the human nature that can not be codified.

The Feudal Lord divided humanity and the world into warring armies of pillage and created nationality as his most potent psychological weapon. His propaganda machine cultivates the ignorance that engenders the nationals. Convincing them that they belong to a State to which they owe the value of their identity, they become the lord's mechanical

---

[12] "The USA PATRIOT Act is an Act of Congress that was signed into law by President George W. Bush on October 26, 2001." - Wikipedia

---

soldiers. The false consciousness of identity of the nationals enables the lord to use them in his wars against his enemies.

His aides—politicians, priests, and generals—wrap the dehumanizing concept in question with patriotism as the glorification of the history of violence of a country that they call the "greatest" in the world.

The lords of capital, land, food, housing, and the rifle use the State to keep the allegiance of their servants—workers, soldiers, politicians, priests, intellectuals, artists, and scientists—under the threat of treason.

The State—through its propaganda machine—converted nationality into an unnatural identity, an object of pride, an obligation to pay tribute, and a duty to make war and kill other serfs in defense of the lords' honor and value of the nationality they own.

The serfs' mind is the incubator of the pride and hate, the instruments with which the lords stimulate their loyalty. The National

Socialist German Workers Party's propaganda machine used the illusion called National Pride as the psychological weapon with which it convinced the German nation to commit genocide against the Jewish people and others [13] in defense of the "purity" of their national origin. The illusion became hate in the mind of the people who believed it was real and a justification for killing other human beings.

The State keeps the Feudal Lord's serfs captured in the illusion of *like being* the owners of a *sort of* Disney World whose wealth and Government they do not possess. The State's propagandists maintain the delusion with speeches exalting nationality, espionage, ballots, bullets, anthems, flags, fireworks, and gory fairy tales of war and heroism.

---

[13] « A broader definition of the Holocaust includes the murder of the Roma and the "incurably sick." A broader definition still includes ethnic Poles, other Slavic groups, Soviet citizens and prisoners of war, homosexuals, Jehovah's Witnesses, black people, and political opponents. » -Wikipedia

The Roots of the Justice System

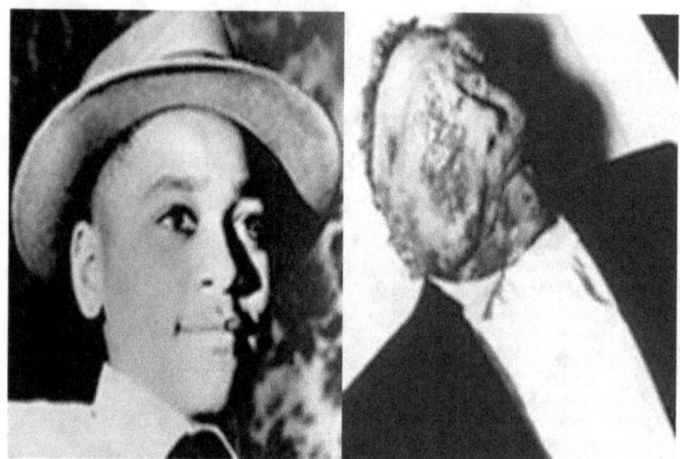

"Emmett Till before and after the lynching on August 28, 1955. He was a fourteen-year-old boy in Chicago who went to spend the summer together with his uncle Moses Wright in Money, Mississippi and was murdered by white men for allegedly assaulting at a white woman. In 2017, the woman told the Associated Press that she had lied about Till whistling at her." -Wikipedia

In capitalism—a society dominated by a class of corporate predators—justice is the effect of the exercise of the power that the people need to defend themselves from the social injustice that the predators create. If the people do not oppose resistance, the justice system—which functions according to the predators' law—will trap them and consume them.

The American justice system emerged from the power of the slave masters who were the law, judges, and executioners of justice. They comprised the system that was adequate to their condition as predators that fed on the bodies of slaves. The Honorable Masters practiced their law by mob lynching. With that brutal method, they created the model of justice that is the root of the synthetic country called America.

The invaders who ignited the enduring genocide of the Native American nations to steal their land incorporated into their State Constitutions the ownership of slaves as a sacred private property right, preserved by God, the State, and the Church.

The slaver did not treat the slave as a person endowed by nature with the natural properties of sensibility, freedom, and equality. The furious lynch mob in the masters' *CIRCUS MAXIMUS* impressed the mind of the white American children with the image of justice exercised with libertinage, and mad savagery. The children who were wet-nursed by African women were taken by their parents to see the hanging of African persons as the representation of an act of justice and amusement that made the family picnic more enjoyable.

The slave master designed the American sense of justice with the image of the tongue of an African man pushed out of his mouth by the force of his body hanging from the lynch mob's rope and the scent of black burnt skin on their pyre.

The lynch mob is the model—a volatile mixture of ignorance, hate, and the pleasure of violence—that the invaders of America used to construct the feelings of self-righteousness and love for the "one nation under God" that they superimposed over the bones of the Native American and African nations.

The perception of justice is still affected by the hallucinations of the master caste: god, country, race supremacy, and power. That is the reason jurors continue to find the African American victims of crimes inspired by slavery guilty of not looking white.

The Bourgeoisie's Directives

The bourgeoisie is the dominant class of society because it can defeat its enemies—particularly the working class—in the daily fight to appropriate the largest portion of society's wealth. Its success is due to the effectiveness of its directives to the State on how to prevent the workers from taking possession of the wealth they produce and emancipating themselves.

The bourgeoisie's directives to the State are the following:

1. Terrorize them.
2. Declass them.
3. Eliminate their will to power.
4. Confuse them.
5. Indoctrinate them with the beliefs that a god created them; their suffering is the consequence of their sin; their dispossession is beatitude; the solution to their oppression is "eternal salvation;" the labor concentration camps in which they are exploited are their countries; they owe allegiance and tribute to the

State for its protection, and they must fight in the bourgeoisie's for-profit wars to defend the emptiness of creed and national pride.

6. Segregate them.
7. Don't allow them to take possession of the wealth they produce.
8. Inject them with the feeling of inferiority.
9. Opiate them.
10. Change their vision with television.
11. Massify their senses.
12. Uniform their habits.
13. Keep them in a state of anxiety.
14. Offer them credit.
15. Excite their faith in the resurrection.
16. Sell them crucifixes, flags, and prayers.
17. Make them feel that their life depends on the men of god and the armed forces.
18. Terrorize them.

Injustice Cannot Engender Justice

The killing of Michael Brown Jr. [14] by a policeman has been converted by the Corporate Media (CM) into the question of whether the

---

[14] "Michael Brown Jr. (May 20, 1996 – August 9, 2014) graduated from Normandy High School in St. Louis County eight days before his death." -Wikipedia

demanders of justice in Ferguson, Missouri, are acting peacefully or violently.

Michael's killer, Darren Dean Wilson—an employee of the Ferguson Police Department with a publicly funded salary and gun—was not indicted. [15]

In the year of the killing of Michael, 2014, the following people were also killed by police, according to the list published by GAWKER on December 8, 2014:

- Rumain Brisbon, 34, Phoenix, Ariz.—Dec. 2, 2014
- Tamir Rice, 12, Cleveland, Ohio—Nov. 22, 2014
- Akai Gurley, 28, Brooklyn, NY—Nov. 20, 2014
- Kajieme Powell, 25, St. Louis, Mo.— August 19, 2014

---

[15] "A grand jury was called and given extensive evidence from Robert McCulloch, the St. Louis County Prosecutor. On November 24, 2014, McCulloch announced the St. Louis County grand jury had decided not to indict Wilson (Darren Dean)." -Wikipedia

- Ezell Ford, 25, Los Angeles, Calif.—August 12, 2014
- Dante Parker, 36, San Bernardino County, Calif.—August 12, 2014
- John Crawford III, 22, Beavercreek, Ohio—August 5, 2014
- Tyree Woodson, 38, Baltimore, Md.—August 2, 2014
- Eric Garner, 43, New York, N.Y.—July 17, 2014
- Victor White III, 22, Iberia Parish, La.—March 22, 2014
- Yvette Smith, 47, Bastrop, Texas—February 16, 2014
- McKenzie Cochran, 25, Southfield, Mich.—January 28, 2014
- Jordan Baker, 26, Houston, Texas—January 16, 2014

The CM's interest is not to investigate the truth, nor expose it as it is found, without prejudice, or emotional insinuation. The reason is the "news" heralds serve the need of the State—which protects the barons who own the news factories—to keep the taxpaying slaves—

notably the oppressed African American Nation—at peace with oppression.

The keeping of the bankers' peace of business, as usual, is the CM's and the State's common preoccupation. They are not in the business of cultivating the truth so that it can flourish into justice. For the usurers who control the life of the dispossessed African American communities, the value of a human being's life is equal to the interest they can pay on a loan. The exploiters of human beings have infected the mind of the police with their depreciation of the natural value of humanity's life.

The consequences of injustice cannot engender justice. This is the problem that remains unsolved: the slave masters built America's justice system with the blood and the bones of the Native Americans and African slaves. They killed natives and slaves impelled by their desire to possess land and wealth as the realization of their right. Negating the human condition of their victims' life and their rights, they formed their awareness of justice.

The mob that lynched natives and slaves was the first American court of justice. It was the consequence of the war that the invaders waged without any human, moral, religious, or legal restraint to realize their ambition. Lynching was the means that fit their end, that is, the invasion of the mind of their victims to impose racial supremacy, terror, fear, and death on them. Mob lynching engendered the Jim Crow [16] laws with which the State created an apartheid order to continue the slavery of Native Americans and African Americans without chains.

The justice that the Civil Rights Act of 1964 represents emerged from the terror that the

---

[16] "Jim Crow laws were state and local laws that enforced racial segregation in the Southern United States. Enacted by white Democratic-dominated state legislatures in the late 19th century after the Reconstruction period, these laws continued to be enforced until 1965. In 1877, a national Democratic Party compromise to gain Southern support in the presidential election resulted in the government's withdrawing the last of the federal troops from the South. White Democrats had regained political power in every Southern state.[3] These Southern, white, Democratic Redeemer governments legislated Jim Crow laws, officially segregating black people from the white population."

-Wikipedia

Ku Klux Klan and the police opposed to the African American people who demanded equality and equal rights in a society whose Government claimed to be a democracy.

The Supreme Court of today is the successor of the justices who upheld the institution of slavery and, thus, the practice of injustice as justice. [17] Today's magistrates administer a justice system that grew from the dominant relation of the masters' class with the rest of society.

Judges are a privileged caste whose mentality the think tanks called universities mold according to the interests of their donors: the thieves who stole the country. Their mission is to defend the property rights that the robbers obtained stealing, killing, and lying. The magistrates' moral imperative is maintaining the power system—the private property of the

---

[17] "The three most important Supreme Court Justices before the Civil War—Chief Justices John Marshall and Roger B. Taney and Associate Justice Joseph Story—upheld the institution of slavery in ruling after ruling." -Supreme Injustice: Slavery in the Nation's Highest Court by Paul Finkelman

resources and means of production stolen from society—which the judges and their bosses use to live as the opulent beneficiaries of inequality and injustice.

The killing of Michael Brown Jr. was another product of the police justice machine that the creators of the injustice of slavery built. An element of the machine killed him as an African American youth living in a society where the police force that surveils the life of the dispossessed African American communities behaves as a "slave patrol." [18]

The justice machine reacted with the prejudice that it teaches its agents to identify the "suspect," their "suspicious skin," and "suspicious conduct." The machine operators installed a behind-closed-doors grand jury of three black and nine white members who decided that the expropriation of Michael Brown Jr.'s life did not warrant the indictment of the expropriator.

---

[18] "Slave patrols and centralized municipal policing were both known for their brutality and ruthlessness." -Center for American Progress: "The Intersection of Policing and Race"

Soldier: Don't Wage War!

Soldier, you must know this:

War is not a patriotic act! It is a brutal act and an irreparable crime against humanity! When you make war, you kill, are killed or become an incurable victim of the orgy of killing. You suffer a lifetime of nightmares produced by the violent alteration of the normal functioning of your neurons at the war indoctrination camp and the battlefield. The shock of battle does not dispel after you have completed your killing tour, even if your instigators give you a medal for bravery. The fear and aggressiveness that drive you in combat are encoded by your neurons permanently.

The cruelty that comprises the war environment becomes a pattern that continues to influence your behavior after the explosions, screaming, bleeding, and dying has ended. Outside that field of high tension and insecurity—in which you feel under control because you are holding your weapon—, you feel maladapted and dysfunctional. You start to wonder why you do not feel satisfied with the war you made to preserve the peace, as your commander told you, that now seems to cause anxiety to you. Something happens to you that you cannot explain.

Contrary to the suggestion of invincibility that your instigators implant on your mind, you feel confused, insecure, and vulnerable. You ask the government that ordered you to make war for an explanation of your condition. Instead of telling you the truth, they prescribe you drugs to numb your feelings of horror for the rest of your life. You become addicted to the peace drugs, but you still cannot be at peace with yourself.

Agitation starts to compel you to recreate the war scenarios that you experienced. You commit reflex acts of violence that produce the depression that stimulates you to commit suicide.

War is not a human need. Its effects do not satisfy the conditions for living a peaceful, altruist, and prosperous life. The State and the Church have falsified the true cannibal nature of war glorifying it as an act of rationality, patriotism, and faith.

The truth is war is a business conducted by the State on behalf of the plutocracy who lives off the pillage. The plutocrats sell everything that is needed to make a war: advertisement, lies, the image of the enemy, fear, suspicion, hate, weapons, chemicals, technologies, drugs, reconstruction materials, and loans for reconstructing the countries they destroy.

"The U.S. government spent $598.5 billion, over half of its discretionary budget, on military and weapons technology in 2015. Virginia-based Lockheed Martin's arms sales totaled $36.44 billion in 2015, by far the most of any company." [19]

The plutocracy destroyed the economy that sustained the life of the U.S. working class. They do not invest in the development of the domestic economy because they decided that it is not a profitable business for them anymore. That is the reason they make war to destroy other peoples and countries, to create business opportunities and live off the victims of war. The plutocrats commit that crime because they are a parasitic class, without allegiance to god or country, driven by avarice, selfishness, and indifference to the human suffering they cause. Their insatiable desire for money compels them to compete for the dominance of the business world they have built at the expense of the pain and death of the impoverished majority of humanity.

The U.S. Government is the plutocracy's war manager, and you are their cannon fodder. When you make war, you become a predator of

---

[19] **"20 companies profiting the most from war" -24/7 Wall St., 5/31/2017**

your species with a mission to inflict terror, suffering, and death on people you do not know. Your actions in combat do not produce food for the hungry, employment for the unemployed, medical care for the ill, or housing for the homeless. In this sense, you become part of the plutocracy's cruelty and indifference when you make their war.

The New American Dronecracy

The U.S. Government is a warring organism that evolved from the traits of the invaders of America—avarice, mistrust, racism, and hostility—and the genocidal way in which they practiced the reason for their pilgrimage to the new continent.

The criminals who appropriated the Native Americans' land created the Government in response to their need for having a fortress and an army to defend their loot as private property. Thus, "the founding fathers" transformed themselves into the prototype of property owners. Consequently, their practice of right and justice became an emanation of their violent psyche.

The Government made war against the Native Americans to take away their power, reduce them, and confine them to concentration camps to impose its supremacy on them. War was also the mentality and method that the State used to segregate the survivors of the African slaves under a law that the Ku Klux Klan imposed with terror. Death by mob lynching of Native Americans and African Americans was the method that the American Masters practiced for developing the sense of justice that they needed to maintain their power.

The fury and fire that the invaders used to force the birth of America became the mood of their Government and the fabric of its foreign policy. The atomic bombing of Hiroshima and Nagasaki and the poisoning of Vietnam with Agent Orange are examples of the enhancement of the violence that engendered the Manifest Destiny.

The Government's proclamation of trust in God "the all merciful"—written on the $1.00 bill—does not guarantee its morality. No belief which may affect its function conditions its conscious. The statesmen believe whatever is necessary to enhance the power of the ruling class they serve. Harry S. Truman, a Baptist Democrat, explained it in the following terms: *"The atom bomb was no 'great decision.' It was merely another powerful weapon in the arsenal of righteousness."*

Truman subjected the killing of thousands of human beings to the Government's necessity for imposing its self-attributed good on Japan and the world. In fact, the use of the atom bomb was a test of a new weapon that stimulated the growth of the military-industrial complex as a model of government and democracy.

The usurers and the weapons manufacturers—who supply the Government's war machine—are the force that determines its morality and policy. Their agents in The Cabinet design the ideological, economic, and military plans to keep humanity at war, starving, ill, dying, and dominated by client-governments that buy their ideas, loans, and weapons.

The public officials extirpated the people, peace, and prosperity, from their conscious to convert it into the incubator of the corruption of the plutocracy who lives off the pillage of war. Democrats and Republicans changed the Government's purposes to the purchasing and selling of military equipment, and conducting the for-profit wars financed by the bankers [20].

---

[20] "In the beginning of World War, I, Woodrow Wilson had adopted initially a policy of neutrality. But the Morgan Bank, which was the most powerful bank at the time, and which wound up funding over 75 percent of the financing for the allied forces during World War I, pushed Wilson out of neutrality sooner than he might have done, because of their desire to be involved on one side of the war." -Bankers Hate Peace: All Wars Are Bankers' Wars, Global Research

Congress' moral justification for its existence is to satisfy the ruling class' demands. Representatives and Senators use the people's Government to embrace the properties of their Wall Street donors—ignorance, parasitism, avarice, Roman opulence, supremacy, racism, belligerence, sterility, and mediocrity—as the national values.

The plutocracy is the model of power and corruption that stimulates the ambitions of the parasitic caste of the career politicians. They educate the new generations to regard the ruling class as the benefactor of their country without whom it cannot be great, and they cannot feel proud of it. The Democrats and Republicans—through their ideological machine—teach the new generations that lie is the truth, corruption is honesty, capitalism is a democracy, security is a police state, and war is the practice of reason.

The fusion of the plutocrats' and public officials' corruption was revealed by their alliance to pillage the Public Treasury after the Wall Street Cartels pushed the nation into the *subprime mortgage crisis*. The Republican Party and the Democratic Party formed a Patriotic United Front to rescue the usurers from the crisis they created, armed with the Emergency Economic Stabilization Act of 2008 [21]. The bailout of the capitalist thieves was an effect of the previous elimination of the Federal Banking Regulations that protected the people from the greed of the bankers who pushed them into a self-consuming debt.

The Democrat and Republican lawmakers showed that they are equal servants of one master, the plutocracy, to whom they pay allegiance. They did not save the victims of the predatory lenders. Consequently, they were evicted [22], *en masse*, by the judges and sheriffs who operate the usurers' legal guillotine.

---

[21] "Law enacted in response to the subprime mortgage crisis authorizing the United States Secretary of the Treasury to spend up to $700 billion to purchase distressed assets, especially mortgage-backed securities, and supply cash directly to banks." -Wikipedia

[22] "Since 2007, the foreclosure crisis has displaced at least 10 million people from more than 4 million homes across the country." -The Nation: "The Great Eviction"

The Representatives and Senators are the columns that support the throne of corruption of the plutocracy. It is the class they recognize as the embodiment of providence and American Exceptionalism. Thus, they cannot have an ethical contract with the people, be sensible to their claims, and solve the social problems that the ruling class creates, such as homelessness, hunger, illness, drug addiction, prostitution, violence, illiteracy, and suicide. Feeling compassion for the suffering that their sponsored subsidy of the banking and war industries causes is not the reason for the public officials' imperial salaries.

The maintenance of the for-profit war industry and the purchasing of its products for killing life and destroying Earth is the function of the Government. One of such products is the Unmanned Combat Aerial Vehicle (UCAV), also known as a combat drone. The cost of 1 MQ-9 Reaper drone was, approximately, $19.5 million per unit in 2016 [23]. The Government subtracts the

---

[23] "Why the World's Most Expensive Drone Costs $19 Million" -24/7 Wall St

value of upgrading the lethal capacity of the war machine from the working class' food budget.

In response to the Military-Industrial Complex (MIC) pressure, the Democrat and Republican lawmakers forced the people into becoming the MIC's most loyal and wealthiest client. And they also embraced the MIC's profit-making mission as part of their oath of loyalty to the State. Superimposing the war budget over the welfare budget, Congress has transformed America into a dronecracy [24] whose self-given mission is imposing the American spirit on the world via the new war strategy imposed by the for-profit drone industry. The need to keep the State's war machine running at home and on its bases in the countries dominated by the plutocracy determines the policy of the new form of government based on the interest that the MIC embodies.

Barack Hussein Obama II—the Nobel Peace Prize winner of 2009—is the leader of the

---

[24] A Government based on the power of a war weapon and whose policy is influenced by the weapon's manufacturers. Harry S. Truman's Government was an atomicracy.

new American dronecracy and the Hope of winning the "War on Terror" by investing public money in the purchasing of drones to satisfy the MIC's avarice. His Government's budget proposal for 2011 included $548.9 billion [25] for the Department of Defense. The Democrats' and Republicans' justification for their aggressive policy is that "America Must Always Lead" the world. Incapable of leading the people—at home or abroad—with morality, rationality, fairness, and persuasion, they adopted the MIC as the oracle that guides them.

The Drone Budget is a war budget for war is the profit-making mission of the MIC. It is not a budget for defending the people from the hidden domestic enemy called hunger.

"In 2010, 48.8 million Americans lived in food insecure households, meaning they were hungry or faced food insecurity at some point during the year. That's 12 million more people than faced hunger in

---

[25] **"Obama's Budget Calls for Billions in New Spending for Drones" -Truthout**

2007, before the recession, and represents 16.1 percent of the U.S. population." [26]

The purpose of the Obama Dronecracy is not only to enrich the war merchants but to validate the use of the drone as a *"powerful weapon in the arsenal of righteousness"* as Harry S. Truman said about the atomic bomb. The State's purpose is to use the drone in the ruling class' domestic war against the suspects of "un-American activities" and immigrant workers. Dissenting, whistleblowing, and opposing the plutocracy's dispossession of the people of their natural heritage and destruction of Earth are democratic rights that the Obama Drone Government treats as treason.

Wall Street and the MIC converted the Democratic State into a Warring State they use to free themselves from regulation and subject the people's interest to their greed. The State's military weight has stressed society into a social crisis driven by the for-profit wars budget and its consequences: unemployment, homelessness,

---

[26] **"Hunger in America" -Center for American Progress**

hunger, prostitution, drug addiction, mental illness, racism, and violence.

The plutocracy has obscured the social crisis they have created and expiated themselves from responsibility with the lawmakers' absolution. Their propagandists have diverted the attention of the people that they have dispossessed from them as the cause of their suffering. The plutocrats' purpose is to adjust the Warring State to the social crisis so that it can keep the people submitted to their for-profit war agenda, law, and order.

Congress' reaction to the social crisis has been to submit it to the National Security Agency (NSA) for management under the terms of the USA/Patriot Act [27], the legal weapon of the domestic War on Terror.

---

[27] "The USA PATRIOT Act is an Act of Congress that was signed into law by President George W. Bush on October 26, 2001. On May 26, 2011, President Barack Obama signed the PATRIOT Sunsets Extension Act of 2011, a four-year extension of three key provisions in the Act: roving wiretaps, searches of business records, and conducting surveillance of "lone wolves"—individuals suspected of terrorist-related activities not linked to terrorist groups." -Wikipedia

With the help of their congressional lackeys, the usurers and war merchants have transformed the War on Terror into a domestic political war against the working class, immigrant workers, and dissenters. The Warring State conducts the war—covered with the banner of the national security—with self-given righteousness, lies, fear, political repression, and secrecy. Its objective is to defeat the people by disarming them of their will to power, that is, to constitute themselves as their Government.

Under the Obama Dronecracy—the replacement of the *Obama Government of Hope* charade—the drone merchants' lawyers have become the writers of bills that Congress approves and converted society into the market for their clients' militaristic, and anti-democratic product.

"Toward these and other ends, Congress has authorized putting up to 30,000 drones in U.S. skies within the next eight years. That is to say, Congress passed the bill. Lobbyists from the Association for

Unmanned Vehicle Systems International openly took credit for having written it." [28]

The Drone-in-Chief Obama has led the for-profit drone wars—incited by the MIC and sponsored by Congress—in which thousands of people have been killed, including innocent children.

"According to the ODNI [Office of the Director of National Intelligence] report, between Jan. 20, 2009, and Dec. 31, 2015, there were 473 strikes that killed between 2,372 and 2,581 combatants and between 64 and 116 noncombatants. According to the averages within the ranges provided by the New America Foundation, Long War Journal, and the Bureau of Investigative Journalism (found here), as of Friday President Barack Obama has actually been responsible for 528 strikes that killed 4,189 persons, an estimated 474 of whom were civilians." [29]

---

[28] **"Drones in U.S. Flight Paths: What Could Go Wrong?" - TheHumanist.com**
[29] **"Do Not Believe the U.S. Government's Official Numbers on Drone Strike Civilian Casualties" -FP (Foreign Policy)**

Furthermore, the pilots who fly the drones and execute the killing of human beings are becoming victims of "friendly fire" in the drone wars that they are fighting. Posttraumatic stress disorder (PTSD) is driving some of them to commit suicide as part of the number of casualties that war causes outside the field of combat.

"According to the most recent report published by the VA [U.S. Department of Veterans Affairs] in 2016, which analyzed 55 million veterans' records from 1979 to 2014, the current analysis indicates that an average of 20 veterans a day die from suicide." [30]

The new American dronecracy is the form of government that evolved from warfare as the principal business of the plutocracy managed by the State on their behalf. Furthermore, Congress' War on Terror, the invention of the drone, and the Department of Defense acceptance of the drone as a "surgical strike" instrument provoked the ongoing transformation of the

---

[30] **"United States military veteran suicide" -Wikipedia**

Government into the administrator of a for-profit war machine.

The leader of the dronecracy is the MIC whose lobby exercises the influence that produces the lawmakers' decisions that sustain war as the condition of its existence. The purpose of the drone Government is to serve the merchants of death by purchasing their product, selling it, and using it in the wars that produce the profits that feed the insatiable avarice of the usurers and arms dealers.

The dronecracy is the result of the defeat that the plutocracy inflicted on the people, particularly the working class, as the controller of the power of the Government. That is the reason Congress became the servant of the MIC and fertile mind for the growth of the dictatorship of the plutocracy it represents.

The consent of the people who support it with their vote and tax—particularly the workers organized in labor unions—determines the dronecracy's ability to function as a machine that produces their suffering. Since the plutocracy defeated the workers [31], they have submitted themselves to their defeat—as a foot adapts to a shoe that is shorter than its natural length—under the leadership of a dumb, fat, and wealthy labor bureaucracy which is the manager of the dronecracy's anti-labor policy in the labor unions.

Unwilling to rise to overcome their defeat—breaking their relation with the plutocracy's parties and the labor bureaucracy—the workers have become the supporters of the war chests and capitalist-warmongering mentality of the public officials that they elect. The workers' submission to the decisions that Representatives and Senators make against their interests enables the dronecracy to function as a "managed democracy" (Sheldon Sanford Wolin: Inverted Totalitarianism).

---

[31] One of the workers' historic defeats was the elimination of the Professional Air Traffic Controllers (PATCO) Union in 1981. Ronald Wilson Reagan ordered the firing of the 13,000 union members who had gone on strike to protest against inhuman working conditions. The PATCO leadership had endorsed Reagan as the Republican Party's candidate for President in the 1980 election.

The dronecracy is not a Government of the working class with a policy to eradicate the problems caused by the plutocracy and their capitalist system of wage slavery. On the contrary, its consciousness is a reflection of the plutocracy's predatory condition, which compels them to use the workers as their prey and the country as their hunting territory. Consequently, the dronecracy relates to the workers only to collect their tax, evict them when they don't pay the landlord rent, and punish them when they rebel.

The workers do not have a Government or public servants. The plutocracy has expropriated the country and the State from them. The workers have only themselves to get what they need to live according to their human and constitutional rights. Thus, they must take the public power that they support to represent and serve themselves. Otherwise, the dronecracy will continue to starve them and punish them when they say they are hungry.

About the Author

Biographic Notes

I Am a DNA Specimen

I am a Deoxyribonucleic acid (DNA) specimen who evolved on Earth from stardust and bacterium, approximately, 3 billion years ago.

Life and the law of natural selection transformed my ancestors into Homo Erectus. Led by their curiosity about themselves and the universe, they created fire and the first tools of cognition. The intellect that they developed and transferred to my genes transformed me into a Homo Sapiens.

When the world excites my curiosity, I can ratiocinate, discern, and laugh, para-normally in the dark, like a child entrapped by his fascination with dementia.

1. Birth

My mother told me that she gave birth to me in the room where she lived with my older brother, Franklin Bartolomé Gómez Sequeira, in the Santa Lucía ghetto of the City of Granada, Nicaragua, Central America. Her neighbor gave her first aid until my maternal grandmother, Dolores (Mama Lola) Lacayo de Sequeira, arrived and helped her deliver me. At midday, I came out of her uterus yawning and hungry. My Mama Lola severed my umbilical cord and buried it in a hole in the Earth, without a marker, on March 12, 1949.

After I had turned three years old, without having spoken any of the words of childhood, my mother told me that she started to fear that I, perhaps, was born mute. To solve her doubt, one day she put me to the test, to see how I would react. She did not give me the bottle of milk at the time on which I was accustomed to receiving it. "Then, you came to me, pulled my dress, and told me: 'Mama, milk.' And this is how I found out that you were normal."

"One day [mother continues telling me the story of my childhood] you drank from the tin where I kept the creolin because you were a glutton and, perhaps, you thought it was milk [creolin changes color, from blackish-brown to white, when it is mixed with water]. However, thanks to God, you did not die."

2. Memories

A Wild Plant

I grew up, accidentally, like a wild plant, in La Otra Banda, a *reducción* (reduction) that the Spanish Empire and Catholic Empire built in Granada to intern the dispossessed survivors of their war of conquest and pillage against the indigenous nations. It was part of the remains of the *encomienda and Indian reductions plan* that the Spanish Empire's soldiers, *encomenderos* (trustees of land and native slaves), and *curas doctrineros* (the doctrinaire catholic priests) executed in Nicaragua. The reduced natives were the basis of the Xalteva Church: A source of forced faith, labor, and payment of tribute to a monarchy whose colonialist descendants still live off the wealth that they inherited from the genocide and the larceny that their ancestors committed against the indigenous nations.

After my mother had impregnated me with her blood, the Church and the State marked me as their farm animal with the same iron of identification with which they had imprinted my parents and grandparents: proletarian. Thus, the bourgeoisie maintained its false sense of identity pure as the ruling class; its life differentiated from the existence of the proletariat as an already identified enemy, and its power intact.

The purpose of the reduction was to serve as the physical, psychological, and cultural reducer of the natives' life. The *encomenderos* and *curas doctrineros* demarcated their space with the whip, the crucifix, punishment, and fear. Thus they implanted in the reduced natives' mind the illusion that God had created the rich and the poor. The *curas doctrineros'* sermon exalted the natives' dispossession as a condition that earned them the sympathy of God. The elements of the natives' world that the catholic colonialists created were dispossession, obscurantism, illiteracy, superstition, alcoholism, violence, confession, punishment, and the fear of the God that the Spanish Army had imported to Nicaragua as a war weapon.

The confession of faith in God and Somoza was the norm within which the *curas doctrineros* and the National Guardsmen had framed the lives of the natives who had been conquered to enlarge the coffers of Spain and the Vatican. Superstition mixed with the unequal economic struggle against the bourgeois and clerical parasites to survive was the reducer of their need to overthrow the reduction and act as the historical subjects of reality, that is, life as a natural, sensual, scientific, and political event.

The relationship between the oppressors and the oppressed of Granada—under One God made in Rome and One Dictator made in the U.S.—that engendered me was the same during the colonial period. The conquerors instituted themselves as the reason and moral for the existence of the conquered that they consumed throughout their generations. My maternal grandparents also lived in La Otra Banda as the inheritors of the dehumanizing effects of the war of economic, mental and cultural dispossession, and enslavement that the Spanish Empire and the Catholic Empire unleashed against Nicaragua in 1522.

The Pacific Railway of Nicaragua

One of the memories of the life that I lived in Granada, Nicaragua, is the station of the Pacific Railway of Nicaragua. There, Montenegro, my coworker, and I boarded the train's third-class carriage in the early morning, together with the peasants who, like us, were going to sell their products in the towns whose territories were crossed by the train tracks.

For us, the kids who were studying at the Padre Misieri Elementary School—which was a neighbor of the train station—the train was like a giant horse with wheels that had evolved in the imagination of humanity. It stimulated our joy when we heard the sound of its whistle and the roar of its engine announcing its return from Corinto.

After having been dismissed from the afternoon session classes, we ran towards the train station, jumped into its cars, and joined it in its final trip to the warehouse located at the Lake Nicaragua pier. When the workers had finished unloading the goods that the train brought in its wagons and depositing them in the repository, the machinist operated the locomotive in reverse until we arrived at the turntable at the train station. There, we helped the driver to turn the locomotive's head for its journey back to the depots of the North on the next morning.

The train arrived in Granada as a noble ambassador that crossed the *Coalbrookdale Iron Bridge* in England to bring the news of the fire of the industrial revolution that the proletariat had ignited in Europe. Its fiery and sonorous head came full of dreams, games, romances, and progress for the pillaged nation. It was a historical monument to the proletariat for its contribution to the development of the transportation of production and efficiency in the satisfaction of the needs of society. The progress of the nation—especially of the working family who looked after the train—depended on the preservation and development of it as part of the culture of a country that had been looted and kept in backwardness. The reactionary bourgeoisie that the Spanish, Catholic, and Yanqui empire engendered, saw the train only as a commodity that did not produce surplus value.

Although the workers had built it as a ship to travel to the future—with vision, determination, and steel—the train became a fragile object in the hands of Adolfo Díaz Recinos who was a trusted bandit of the White House and the Holy See. As a member of the Conservative Party, Díaz Recinos took the power of the State in 1911 with the backing of the Colonialist Catholic Church (CCC) and the U.S. Marine Corps, whose violent intrusion in the life of Nicaragua he requested.

As the former secretary of the La Luz and Los Angeles Mining Company—owned by James Gilmore Fletcher and his brothers, G. Fred & D. Watson Fletcher, and Henry P. Fletcher—, Diaz Recinos helped the Yankee pirates steal the gold from the mines of the nation. His treacherous relationship with Nicaragua was the product of his lack of a sense of self, independence, character, and political morality. Being a house servant of Yankee pirates was his source of self-realization and pride.

Unlike Augusto César Sandino, Díaz Recinos did not have the sense of dignity nor did he understand it as the principal value of the nation. Therefore, he handed control of the finances of the State and the train to the bandits Brown Brothers & Company and J. & W. Seligman & Company as security for loans to consolidate the State debt. Following his example, the Conservative, Liberal, and Sandinista politicians that have succeeded him in the Government have not rejected the collection of the odious debt as the exercise of a national liberation duty. On the contrary, they continue to indebt and sell the country as a profitable commodity.

The Conservative Party undermined the future of the train as a social good and stimulus for the development of the nation, which was supported by the faithful work of the proletariat. The Yankee imperialist usurers infected the minds of their Nicaraguan *encomenderos* (their trusted bandits, *vendepatrias* or traitors, in the Government) with their modus operandi: bribery, fraud, lying, and aggressing. The usurers converted their Nicaraguan henchmen into the transmitters of the political corruption plague that continues to dominate the conduct of the bureaucracy that exploits the Catholic Bourgeois State.

Díaz Recinos created the political mannequin which continues to be the model of conduct that all his successors in the Government have followed. His creeping behavior, shamelessness, lying, stealing, self-indulgence, and social indifference became the characteristics of the new generations of Catholic politicians. Like their Conservative founding father, they do not have character and are corruptible under the heat of the desire for power, fortune, and fame.

The rulers who had the duty of preserving the train continued using it as a pawning object with a value relative to their meanness and political advantage. Therefore, they neglected, dismantled, and, finally, Violeta Barrios Torres de Chamorro—who was the President of Nicaragua in 1994—sold it as scrap metal. Doña Violeta also took the power of the State with the backing of the CCC and the Yankee Empire under the Presidency of George Herbert Walker Bush, a member of the Republican Party. Doña Violeta ended what Díaz Recinos started out with the same *vendepatria* (traitorous) mentality of sacrificing the heritage of the nation to keep fattening the

Yankee imperialist usurers with the bloody payment of interest on the odious debt.

The train was a source of work, life, joy and poetic inspiration for thousands of people. The declaration of love for the train of Norma Ramos—an Agent at the Mateare Station—reveals the feeling that the proletariat had developed for their work instrument and the real motherland consciousness. In the *Canal 10 Nicaragua* interview for the Documentary the Train: On the Rails of Memory, on September 23, 2011, Ms. Ramos said: "It was like my husband, everything, everything to me."

However, the lackeys of the Yankee imperialist usurers, the bourgeoisie, and the Vatican who lived off the State's usufruct eliminated it to comply with the conditions of the army of social extermination called International Monetary Fund (IMF) and World Bank (WB). The politicians that destroyed the value of the train for the life of the proletariat revealed the truth of their consciousness. To them, the national heritage is a merchandise subject to the law of supply and demand. Therefore, love for the motherland and loyalty to her are feelings that are not a condition for their existence. In economic reality, politicians are social parasites who live off the sale of the resources of the country they claim to represent. Love and loyalty are only objects of their demagogic speeches in their political campaigns, driven by their ambition, falsehood, and social indifference.

The Catholic Somoza Dictatorship

I woke up to the cognitive life in a society whose citizens had adapted to living as the indifferent prisoners of the dictatorship of the Colonialist Catholic Church and Anastasio Somoza García, the so-called Tacho. He was another trusted villain of the Holy See and the White House whom they had designated as the overseer of their interests in Nicaragua. Tacho, who had appointed himself General—after failing as a businessman—was the boss of the bourgeois, Catholic, pro-Yankee imperialist, and terrorist Mafia that controlled the life of the nation, the exploitation of the proletariat, and the appropriation of the wealth that the working class produced.

The features of that world—which had been shaped by the violence of the Spanish Empire, the Catholic Empire, and the Yankee Empire—were the social scourges that had formed on the open wounds of the consciousness of the survivors of the Indigenous Holocaust. The empires' armies dehumanized them and attempted to remove their instinct for the freedom to convert them into faithful tributary slaves.

The conditions of the time in which my parents were born —illiteracy, unemployment, impoverishment, alcoholism, prostitution, diseases, social violence, and fear of God and Somoza's National Guard— were exacerbated by the occupation of Nicaragua by U.S. Marine Corps.

The Catholic Somoza Dictatorship shaped the mind of my mother and father with the same mold that the *encomenderos* and *curas doctrineros* used to forge the dispossessed indigenous family model during the colonial period. The native Catholic family was the fuel that sustained the imperial system of exploitation in which parents exploited their children to survive. The dictatorship maintained this kind of family—with obscurantism, faith, and alcohol—to keep the new generations of dispossessed slaves detained in the same social jail in which their parents were born.

My parents did not liberate themselves from the prison of faith in God and the State because they did not build the necessary scientific and revolutionary awareness of themselves, the world, and their relationship with it. Their condition was not the effect of a genetic flaw in the evolution of their perception. Rather, it was the result of the occupation of their minds—and their ancestors' minds—by their colonial oppressors, their religion, and their economy.

The *curas doctrineros* suppressed my progenitors' instinct for freedom and marked their foreheads with the words "Confiteor" and "Creed" as the manifestation of the purpose of their lives. The confession of sin and the declaration of belief in God—the acts of fear that the Holy Inquisition induced in their victims— were the psychological instruments with which the doctrinaire priests reduced their thinking to the most minimal expression of obscurantism. Thus, the Colonialist Catholic Church fulfilled the mission that the Spanish empire entrusted to it which engendered the Catholic Somoza Dictatorship.

My originators' religious slavery was the result of the spiritual defeat of the native nations in the Spanish Empire's and the Catholic Empire's war to dehumanize, dispossess, and convert them into slaves of the Christian salvation tributary system. Granada accepted their condition as the exercise of their freedom of worship. The citizens did not see it as a crime of dehumanization because the Catholic Emotion Machine had replaced their sense of humanity with the image of a crucified stranger. Therefore, my parents became the thoughtless transmitters of the traumas that they absorbed from their relationship with their parents. The context in which the transmission happened was the same: A semi-feudal society controlled by sorcerers armed with crucifixes and illiterate soldiers armed with M1 Garands which the Yankee Empire had donated to the Catholic Somoza Dictatorship.

The method that my progenitors used to relate with me—the imposition of Catholicism, forced labor, physical punishment, contempt, and domestic violence influenced by my father's alcoholism—produced a relationship ruled by patriarchal power, intimidation, superstition, and emotional distance. The way they treated me was a reflection of the whip that the *encomenderos* and *curas doctrineros* used to reduce the indigenous and Afro-descendant nations. The dispossessed family which was thus formed by the Catholic Somoza Dictatorship was the matrix that produced the slaves who supported the base of the pyramid on whose cusp the bourgeoisie, its dictator, and Bishop lived opulently.

Adolescence in a Catholic City

In 1962, I was shaken by the explosion in my testicles of the testosterones which caused the spontaneous downpours of sperm that announced the start of the puberty of my life. I became an adolescent in a Catholic City. The chemical upheaval in my body coincided with the Telstar 1 telecommunications revolution. My adolescence had sprung in a world undergoing the political convulsions caused by the inequality imposed by the Church and the State and the dispossessed people's struggle for survival.

At the White House, John F. Kennedy approved the use of the defoliant Agent Orange in the Yankee Plutocracy's war against the Vietnamese people. Pope John XXIII excommunicated Fidel Alejandro Castro Ruz for supporting a "communist government." And the Sandinista Front for National Liberation endeavored to become a revolutionary force capable of accelerating the speed of the wheel of the cart that carried the effects of Nicaragua's rural life.

Meanwhile, Granada lived as a blessed believer that communicated its concerns through the confessional and the Telegraph. The information generated by the life of the rest of humanity, inventions and revolutions, was censored by the Security Office. It was the main arm of the Catholic, bourgeois, pro-Yankee imperialist, and terrorist dictatorship led by Luis Anastasio Somoza Debayle, the so-called Luisito. He had become the *de facto* President of Nicaragua after his father, Anastasio Somoza García, the so-called Tacho, was executed by Rigoberto López Pérez.

The Telstar 1 transmissions did not touch the citizens' foreheads because they lived like the characters in a series of religious scenes projected on the chimeric space of a stamp. Their behavior did not reveal they knew they were elements of a world that moved and changed. For centuries, the Colonialist Catholic Church (CCC) had conditioned their minds with the Ecclesiastical Calendar and the sound of the bell that called them to the temple to confess their sins, repent, receive penance, and pay the resurrection tithe.

The *curas doctrineros* (the doctrinaire Catholic priests) had transmitted the historical trauma caused by the Spanish Empire's indigenous holocaust through the minds of the new generations of slaves of the Holy See as the unbroken link that had kept them in a state of religious alienation since 1524. After years of ink-on-paper independence from the Spanish Empire, the City had not created an independent life because it had surrendered itself—as a defeated and terrorized animal—to its soul hunters irremediably.

The citizens of Granada lived as an organ attached to the parasitic body of the clergy through the umbilical cord of their concern with guilt for sin, penance, and redemption. Catholic indoctrination had turned them into the objects of their mortification. Their acts of faith before a crucifix were modern forms of human sacrifice to appease the wrath of a God that they did not know but feared and wanted as their redeemer. That conflict kept them in a psychotic state—without signs of vigor or freedom—which was the link of their addiction to the objects of religion. The Colonialist Church had succeeded in replacing the citizens' instinct, that is, the logical operation of their neurons with the dependence of their minds on the hallucinatory rites it conducted.

The struggle of the City's classes for survival did not stimulate their dissent with themselves as the objects of a backward mode of production stimulated with the incense of Catholicism. Bourgeois and proletarians lived in the illusion that they were children of the same Motherland and Holy Mother Church. The static force of religion neutralized the social transformation potential implicit in their class interest and their interaction through the system of production of the nation's wealth.

The result of the illusion was a citizenry suspended in time, like a relic. In the social reality, the proletarians were the survivors of the Indigenous Holocaust that the *encomenderos* and *curas doctrineros* had dispossessed and forced into tributary-slavery. Unlike the bourgeois, the proletarians did not have a political party nor struggled against their class enemies armed with their class consciousness. The conquered and the conquerors participated in the Eucharist and had become the fearful objects of the Catholic

Somoza Dictatorship. Praying "May God's will be done" and kneeling before a doctrinaire priest to accept the impression of an ash cross on their foreheads seemed to transfuse into their minds the sense of equality and peace between them.

The Catholic Somoza Dictatorship's holy men and guardsmen had paralyzed the citizens' free, mundane, and revolutionary instinct with terror. The delusion of guilt for the "original sin" kept them praying "I confess to Almighty God" on their knees in a temple. Superstition had replaced their evolutionary, social need to confront themselves in the mirror of the real world that moved, always driven by hunger, the class struggle for survival, politics, and revolution. With Mass, political repression, and the murder of its political opponents, the dictatorship prevented the transformation of the majority of the citizens' hunger into political consciousness and revolutionary wrath.

Granada was not a City adequate to the revolution of adolescence nor the growth of revolutionary ideas. Historically, its purpose was to serve as the mansion and the garrison of the administrators of the colonial Catholic power. The City was the supervisor of the exploitation of the native slaves, the pillage of Nicaragua, the collection of the tribute, and the repressor of the social overflow.

The young, freethinkers, gay, poetic, and long-haired citizens were repressed by the soldiers of the colonial Catholic morality as a danger to the power of the descendants of the thieves who stole the native nations' land and the spirit of their freedom. The conservative ruling class confronted the youth's impetus for freedom, sexuality, and creativity with the spectacle of the Passion and Independence Day to confuse their desire.

The CCC had converted Granada into a Holy Week Relic that it sold to the resurrection tithe-payers to maintain the power of the Vatican Bank and the College of Cardinals' opulent lifestyle.

3. Education

Diplomas

Elementary School
Escuela Padre Misieri, Granada, Nicaragua

High School
Colegio Salesiano San Juan Bosco, Granada, Nicaragua

Industrial Clerk
Associated Colleges of California, Los Angeles, CA, U.S.

Professional Legal Assistant
American International Career College, San Diego, CA, U.S.

Exams Passed

Civil Service
City of Los Angeles Government, CA, U.S.

Notary Public
State of California Government, U.S.

Translator
Los Angeles City College, Los Angeles, CA, U.S.

Studies

Jurisprudence
Universidad Centroamericana, Managua, Nicaragua

English Language
Alemany Adult High School, San Francisco, CA, U.S.

Associate of Arts Degree
Los Angeles City College, Los Angeles, CA, U.S.

Graphic Design
Los Angeles Trade Technical College, Los Angeles, CA, U.S.

Scholarships

High School
Colegio Salesiano San Juan Bosco, Granada, Nicaragua

Associate of Arts
Los Angeles City College, Los Angeles, CA, U.S.

Prizes

First Place
Catholic Catechism Contest, Granada, Nicaragua

Honor Roll
Colegio Salesiano San Juan Bosco, Granada, Nicaragua

Dean's Honor List
Los Angeles City College, Los Angeles, CA, U.S.

Second Place
English Speech Contest, Los Angeles City College, Los Angeles, CA, U.S.

Student of the Month
American International Career College, San Diego, CA, U.S.

4. Literary Activity

Prizes

Excellence in Poetry Certificate
Awarded by Teresinka Pereira, director of the *International Society of Poetry* and professor of romance languages at the University of Colorado, Boulder, CO, U.S.

First Place in Poetry Contest
Awarded by Lillian Walsh, editor of *For Poets Only*, a poetry magazine published in Jackson Heights, NY, U.S.

Edited Books

Venus Is Bleeding by Roxanna Gómez Sequeira

Please Don't Circumcise My Clitoris by Roxanna Gómez Sequeira

Alice in Weirdland by Roxanna Gómez-Ubau

My Home Cooking by Marie Marín

El Salvador: The Betrayal of the Farabundo Martí National Liberation Front (FMLN) (Spanish Edition) by Armando A. Molina

On the Edge of Silence: My Journey on the Boulder by Rodolfo Sotelo Jr.

Edited Magazines

Censored Poem, Red and Black, Class Struggle, Sacrifice the Common Sense, Electronic Poetry, The Darwinian Primate, Politikos, and *Chemical World*

Contributions

LA Weekly, Los Angeles, CA, U.S.

Free Venice Beachhead, Venice, CA, U.S.

5. Work

Nicaragua

In the City of Granada, HuGóS worked as a seller of flowers and popsicles, shoeshine boy, *Lazarillo* or a boy who guides a blind person, Algebra tutor, newspaper reporter (*El Mundo* or The World), radio announcer (Radio Sport and Radio Granada), and factory worker.

The United States

In the City of San Francisco, CA, HuGóS worked as a dishwashing machine operator in the kitchen of the Fairmont San Francisco Hotel for a salary of $1.00 per hour of work.

In the City of Los Angeles, CA, HuGóS worked as a dishwashing machine operator, stock clerk, factory worker, retail clerk, Notary Public, translator, and Retirement Benefits Specialist.

Public Service

In the City of Los Angeles Government, HuGóS worked in the Retirement Department as a Benefits Specialist for 30 years. In that entity, he counseled the members and beneficiaries of the retirement plan on the provisions of the

Administrative Code for benefits and how to request payment of them. Furthermore, he performed the functions of Legal Assistant, a specialist in the processing of Community Property Division Court Orders, instructor, writer of manuals, Notary Public, and translator.

Community Work

In the City of Los Angeles, HuGóS helped undocumented immigrant workers, in 1987, to understand the terms and conditions of the Immigration Control and Reform Act (IRCA) of 1986 of the Federal Government of the United States. Moreover, he assisted them with the acquisition and translation, from Spanish to English, of the documents required by the law so that they could request amnesty and an immigrant visa.

Work Certificates

Certificate of Excellent Public Service
Awarded by the Los Angeles City Employees' Retirement System, Los Angeles, CA, U.S.

Certificate of Employee of the Quarter
Awarded by the Los Angeles City Employees' Retirement System, Los Angeles, CA, U.S.

Bibliography

Books by HuGóS

In Transition Towards Poetry (Spanish Edition)	1978
What's the Meaning of All This?	1988
I Was Caught in a Cloudy Turbulence	1989
First Amendment: Rejected Stories	1989
When I Was a Boy, I Had Wings	1990
Somnambulist (Spanish Edition)	1990
The Liberation of the Senses	1991
Quando Era Menino Tinha Asas Translation by Teresinka Pereira	1991
It Hurts to Feel	1992
This Life Isn't Mine	1994
Visions of a Somnambulist (Spanish Edition)	2011
In Transition Towards Poetry Granada (Nicaragua), the Bourgeoisie, and the FSLN (Spanish Edition)	2014

Nicaragua: The Dialogue Between the Doctrinaire Priests and the Trustees (Spanish Edition) — 2014

Socialism of the XXI Century or the Anti-revolution (Spanish Edition) — 2016

Notes from My Mobile Brain — 2017

Magazines in Which HuGóS Works Have Appeared

Poema Censurado, Los Angeles, CA, U.S. — 1977

La Prensa Literaria, Managua, Nicaragua — 1977

Poema Convidado, Boulder, CO, U.S. — 1978

Taller, León, Nicaragua — 1978

Rojo y Negro, Los Angeles, CA, U.S. — 1978

L.A. Weekly, Los Angeles, CA, U.S. — 1987

Directory of International Writers and Artists, Moorhead, MN, U.S. — 1988

Mutated Viruses, Chicago, IL, U.S. — 1988

Sacrifice the Common Sense, Los Angeles, CA, U.S. — 1989

For Poets Only, Jackson Heights, NY, U.S. — 1989

The Nocturnal Lyric, Pasadena, CA, U.S. — 1989

Southern Rose Review, Ripley, MS, U.S. — 1989

The Plowman, Ontario, Canada — 1989

Poetry by the Seas, Oceanside, CA, U.S. — 1989

The Aldebaran, Bristol, RI, U.S.	1990
Gypsy, El Paso, TX, U.S.	1990
Poetalk, Berkeley, CA, U.S.	1990
Harvest 15, Boulder, CO, U.S.	1991
Transição, Boulder, CO, U.S.	1991
Ráfagas, Paris, France	1993
Estrella del Sur, Paterna, Valencia, España	1997
Lluvia de Vidrio, Azul, Buenos Aires, Argentina	1997
Poesía Sin Fronteras, Jaén, Andalucía, España	1999
Free Venice Beachhead, Venice, CA, U.S.	2011
mundopoesía.com	2012
allpoetry.com	2017

The Colonialist Catholic Church Abused this Boy

Humberto Gómez Sequeira-HuGóS on the day that his parents delivered him to a doctrinaire priest of the Colonialist Catholic Church, for the administration of the First Communion poisonous vaccine, at the San José Chapel of the San Juan de Dios Hospital. Granada, Nicaragua. Circa 1956.